Crete West

Gert Hirner / Jakob Murböck

Walks in
Western Crete

Translated by Gill Round

52 selected walks
along the coasts and in the mountains of Western Crete

With 70 colour photographs,
52 walking maps 1:50,000 / 1:100,000
and a small contextualising map to a scale of 1:750,000

ROTHER · MUNICH

Front cover:
Countryside near Georgioúpolis and the summit of Kástro
(White Mountains).

Frontispiece (photo on page 2):
The hidden Katholikó monastery in a gorge.

All photographs by the authors

Cartography:
Walking maps 1:50,000 / 1:100,000 © Bergverlag Rother GmbH, Munich
(drawn by CompuMapping Koebele, Dietmannsried),
contextualising maps to a scale of 1:750,000 / 1:2,000,000
© Freytag & Berndt, Vienna

2nd edition 2003
© Bergverlag Rother GmbH, Munich

ISBN 3-7633-4803-4

Distributed in Great Britain by Cordee, 3a De Montfort Street, Leicester
Great Britain LE1 7HD, www.cordee.co.uk

Preface

Western cultural history began on this Mediterranean island when Zeus, transformed into a bull, brought the beautiful goddess Europa to Crete. The last 5,000 years on Crete has seen a blending of eastern Mediterranean culture with that of neighbouring countries and the visitor will sense even today that centuries of history are breathing from every square metre.

Crete is an island for all seasons. An increasing number of visitors are making use of the moderate temperatures in the off-peak months for getting to know the island, the landscapes and the people, and for relaxing too. This is especially true in spring. When snow and rain showers are still sweeping across a winter landscape in middle Europe, the island in spring is already covered with a carpet of colourful blossom. This is the time to pack your rucksack and walking boots and fly off to the sun. There may still be snow on the higher mountains, but the trees in the valleys are resplendent with oranges, while daisies and poppies bring colour to the fields and rare species of orchids are on display for the delight of the hiker. And all around you can hear the sound of sheep bells.

It's the great variety of landscapes which attracts the visitor, characterised by the contrast of mountains and sea. Isolated mountain regions alternate with plateaus, deep ravines, steep coasts, bays and beaches. Walking, therefore, is often the only, and certainly the most intimate, way of getting to know the country and its people and acts as a counter to mass tourism.

The regional diversity and abundance of walks throughout the island make it necessary to divide Crete into areas. The walks are selected in such a way as to take account of different interests in landscape. The suggested walks are thus equally divided between those that go along the sunny coastline and out onto sea-washed peninsulas, and walks to ancient towns in beautiful locations or to ruined monasteries. Other paths lead through the island's mountainous interior, into deep gorges and onto the summits of high mountains. The 52 suggestions for walks are distributed across the most beautiful areas of western Crete and can often be undertaken by families with children.

Many of the walks were carefully checked last year. However, some changes might occur due to new fencing, road building and field construction. The publishers, therefore, would like to ask all visitors to Crete to alert them to any relevant alterations. We hope all users of this guide enjoy many days of adventure amidst the natural beauty of Crete.

Gert Hirner and Jakob Murböck

Contents

Tourist Information

Rock towers on the way to Gíngilos.

Use of the guide
Each walk described in the guide begins with a concise overview of the most important details. All the mountains mentioned, the starting points, the locations and the objectives of every stage of the walk, are contained in the index at the back. There are little maps showing the line of the route and a contextualising map on page 18/19 indicating the location of all the walks.

Grade

The walks are partly along roads and gravel tracks, partly over ground with no paths at all, but mainly on footpaths and tracks. It is mentioned in the text when there are problems with route finding, but the paths are usually straightforward and there are hardly any dangerous places, where, for example, you might fall. However, you should not underestimate the special conditions of the path, like sharp edged rock formations and scree, very prickly undergrowth and lengthy sections over sand and pebbles along the shore, since they make greater demands on fitness and footwear. After prolonged rainfall many paths are either partly, or even totally, impassable and this is indicated in the description. Little-used paths can be completely overgrown in spring, causing problems with route finding. Route numbers are printed in different colours to indicate the level of difficulty and are as follows:

BLUE

These routes are mostly well-marked and only moderately steep, and can be walked safely even in bad weather. They do not usually present any problems with route finding. They can also be undertaken by children and older people without any great danger.

RED

These paths and mountain tracks are, as a rule, well-marked and clearly visible, but frequently narrow and they can be fairly exposed over short sections. They should only be undertaken if you are a sure-footed and fit walker.

BLACK

These mountain routes are often insufficiently marked and are mostly narrow and steep. At times they go over terrain without any paths so that it is essential to have a good sense of direction. These routes should only be attempted if you are an experienced, sure-footed and fit mountain walker and do not suffer from vertigo.

Dangers

Certain sections of exposure, or requiring use of the hands, are mentioned in the text. In some seasons in the mountain regions over 2000m you must be prepared to walk over wide areas of old snow where there's a danger of it giving way. Snowfields frequently cover fissures and caverns – which are typical at these heights – and streams too. Throughout the year, even in fine weather, there's the possibility of strong winds from the south, which can knock down an adult in exposed locations. It is impossible to stand up on the summit in these winds. Especially in north-west Crete there can be heavy storms right up to May. From October onwards this can present unforeseen dangers.

When walking near to villages, isolated farmsteads and outbuildings, you often come across dogs roaming free and sometimes they bark madly and run up to strangers. They are very afraid of stones being thrown and bending down, as if to pick one up, is usually enough to send them packing.

Best seasons

The best conditions for walking are in spring (April / May) and in autumn (September / October). Summer is mostly very hot, but the conditions are excellent for walking in shady valleys and in high altitude mountain areas. Winter is often the best time for walking as there isn't a typical rainy season on Crete. The thermometer quickly climbs to 20°C as soon as the sun shines, but you should also be prepared for two or three days of rain at a time, as well as thunderstorms and snow above 1000m. As a rule, the frequency of rain and low temperatures decreases from the north-west to the south-east and there are regions on the south coast and in the east where you hardly see a drop of rain all year.

Equipment

Sturdy footwear, thick trousers, windproof and waterproof clothing, food, together with enough fluids and sunscreen are essential. When visiting monasteries it is often necessary for women to wear long skirts and to cover their shoulders. Men should wear long trousers.

Maps

There are not at present any walking maps to a scale of 1:50,000 as is common in central Europe. Highly recommended are the Harms-ic 1:100,000 maps of Eastern and Western Crete on which the walks in this guide and the E4 route can be found. However, the scale of the maps is insufficient for detailed route finding.

Walking time

The time details relate to real walking time with a light day-pack and do not include stopping for a rest or to take photos. The length of each stage, the total time, the height variations and sometimes the distances too, are given to help you with the route-finding.

Stops and accommodation

In Crete there are kafenía and tavernas almost everywhere, but only in larger tourist places are there restaurants. It's hardly worth taking food with you on the walks as it is not expensive to stop in the villages for something to eat or drink. Wild camping is possible on Crete due to the mild climate and is tolerated except in a few instances. However, it is not officially allowed and near to villages and tavernas, you should make use of the usually very cheap rooms, giving some consideration to the often impoverished circumstances of the local inhabitants. You can only spend the night in a mountain hut on Crete if you are on a guided walk. Only the Kallérgi hut is staffed from May to October.

Access
There is a good improved public bus network. Many of the starting points can be reached by bus very easily, at least in the tourist season. However, at the beginning and the end of the season and during the Greek summer holidays (July / August) you should double check the times in advance on secondary routes. If you are planning to be off the main roads hire a car, however, the locals will always give you a lift.

Protection of nature and the environment
Crete still has an extensively unspoilt landscape, at least at first glance, but much has changed in recent years with increasing tourism and the developments linked with it. The authorities take little action when there are persistent problems to do with the destruction of the landscape caused either by the building of roads, new hotels and holiday complexes, or by tipping rubbish in the open countryside. Even the Cretans themselves demonstrate an amazingly careless attitude to their country.

In spite of the islanders' apparent lack of concern, we would like to ask you to respect all animal and plant life, to take your rubbish away with you and to be sparing with your use of water. Never throw cigarette ends away carelessly or light an open fire. There's a very real danger of forest fires on the island, particularly at the height of summer and in the autumn. Be careful also when driving a car. There are few restrictions on the road. You come across hire cars in the most unexpected and remote places that are only accessible over rough roads and tracks. And finally, if you see people thoughtlessly destroying the natural surroundings, you might quietly express your surprise.

The E4: the European long-distance path
There's a long-distance footpath across Crete. The black and yellow marked E4, which is divided into about 41 stages, begins in Kastélli Kissamou in the north-west and ends in Káto Zákros in the east. Between Soúgia and Omalós respectively and the Nídha plain there is a south and a north variation, and an increasing number of connecting paths between them. The route goes along old paths and roads, but also sometimes over pathless terrain. Some stages of the E4 are described in this two-volume walking guide as day walks.

Walking in Crete

Geography

With a surface area of 8288km² Crete is the largest of all Greek islands and after Sicily, Sardinia, Cyprus and Corsica, the fifth largest in the Mediterranean. It is 260km long and between 12 and 56km wide. The island is dominated by mountains and hill-country and cut by many deeply fissured ravines that descend to the sea.

Three mountain ranges shape the island – Lefká Ori in the west, 2452m, the Ida massif in the centre, 2446m, and the Díkti mountains in the east, 2148m. In addition there are many other small mountain ranges like the Kouloúkonas mountains on the north coast. In contrast to the mostly steep south coast where access is difficult, the north side consists of mainly flat stretches of coast. The many limestone plateaus which nestle into the mountains are a geological characteristic of Crete. In the west these are the Omalós plateau (2.5km in diameter, 1050 to 1300m high) and the Askífou plateau (1km in diameter, 700m high), and in the centre, the Nídha plateau (1.5km in diameter, 1400m high). They are covered in snow until well into the spring and the meltwater flows through underground stream-systems into the sea, or feeds the few rivers that retain surface water. Lake Kournás is the only freshwater lake on the island.

The island is watered by many reliable springs which have, in the past, been adequate to supply the island's population. However, increasing tourism and the changeover of agriculture to water-intensive cultivation, are necessitating the investigation of new reservoirs. In so doing, more and more caves are being discovered. Over 3000 of them are already known, but very few of them have been fully explored. The heavy usage of water, especially in the summer months, has already led to an obvious lowering of the water table and the drying-up of some wells in many parts of the island.

Flora and Fauna

Crete has 1500 species of plants, of which about 10% are only to be found on this island. The types of trees most prevalent are pines, cypress, holm oaks and scarlet oaks, plane trees and eucalyptus. But the appearance of the landscape is largely defined by cultivated trees: olive, orange, lemon, fig, carob, almond and walnut trees. Near to villages and inland you will also frequently find vineyards.

The tree line is at about 1700m, up to which point there's mainly pasture land with rather sparse vegetation. Herbs thrive here, many of them medicinal. Among them are: sage, thyme, oregano, dittany, rosemary, bayleaf, as well as numerous types of mint. Many kinds of bushes are to be found on the island: oleander, gorse, myrtle, vitex, juniper and many Mediterranean sclerophyllous plants. In winter and spring the wild flowers bloom: narcis-

The Apokorónou district is one of the most well-watered regions in Crete.

sus, alpine violets, anemones, poppies, daisies, and various types of orchid.

The original Cretan fauna is almost extinct. You can still find wild goats, eagles as well as bearded and griffon vultures, all of them protected species. You can also see small animals, rabbits, badgers, turtles, wiesels, hedgehogs, snakes and lizards and numerous species of birds.

Climate and weather

Rainfall is restricted almost totally to the winter months, so that in summer it is mostly dry. The transition periods between these two predominant seasons are accordingly short and often unnoticed. The coldest months are January and February, and the hottest between June and the end of September.

The north is blessed with a somewhat cooler wind in summer, in contrast to the extremely hot south coast. The Sirroco from Africa can be very unpleasant and is often of hurricane force. The temperatures can suddenly increase by 10 degrees and even at night it doesn't get any cooler. Also to be mentioned are the heat storms which occur especially in the north and in the mountains. They can be quite violent and occasionally give advance warning of a few days of bad weather.

History of Crete

6000-2600 BC, Neolithic age: signs of Neolithic settlement on Crete.

2600-2000 BC, Pre-Palace era: migration across the Aegeans onto the plains of central and eastern Crete. Start of working with copper and bronze.

2000-1700 BC, Old Palace period: creation of power centres with palaces in Knossos, Mallia and Festos. Age of cultural ascendancy. Maritime supremacy of the minoans. Lively trade with the Aegian islands, Egypt, North Africa and Asia minor. Upsurge of art and craft. Development of the 'Linear A' script. Destruction of all sites by an almighty earthquake around 1700 BC.

1700-1400 BC, New Palace period: reconstruction of the palaces. Building of the palace at Káto Zákros. High point of art and craft as well as commerce and trade. 'Linear B' script. A volcanic eruption on the island of Santorini around 1450 BC with subsequent earthquakes and seaquakes leads to complete destruction of all palaces and buildings.

1400-1100 BC, Post-Palace period: Doric invaders from the mainland. Surrender of settlements and slavery of local inhabitants. More basic forms now dominate the craft.

1100-67 BC, Doric age: mountain fortresses in Lato, Polirinía, Karfi. Crete becomes part of the Doric settlement. Coins are minted and laws enacted. Trade relations with Phoenix and Egypt. Iron replaces bronze. The 35 states (polis) of Crete feud with one another.

68 BC-395 AD, Roman era: Crete becomes a province of Rome with the centre of Gortys on the Messara plain. Stability and peace now prevail on the island. Concession by Rome for the rights of self-government. Age of economic prosperity. Appearance and spread of Christianity. Following the example of other Roman provinces the building began of roads, bridges, aqueducts, government buildings, temples, theatres, villas and baths.

395-824 AD, first Byzantine era: division of the Roman Empire into east and west. Crete is part of the Byzantine (eastern Roman) empire and does not have any special political role to play. Many churches are built during this time.

824-961 AD, Arab occupation: under the leadership of Abu Hafs Omar, the Arabs (Saracens) land in 824, conquer Gortys and ravage the whole island. Crete becomes a centre of piracy and slave trade in the eastern Mediterranean. Byzantine attempts to conquer the island fail.

961-1204 AD, second Byzantine era: the Byzantine commander, Nikeophoros Phokas, succeeds in driving the Arabs off Crete. Settling of families from all parts of the Byzantine Empire. Immigrants from Genoa and Venice.

1204-1669 AD, Venetian era: in the wake of the 4th crusade Crete falls to Bonifatius II, margrave of Montferrat, who sells it to the Venetians for 10,000 pieces of silver. In 1206 the Venetians land on Crete with 31 ships, colonise the land according to military bases and give the island a new administrative structure.

1669-1898, Ottoman Empire, in spite of great efforts by the Venetians to strengthen their fortification, Hania is conquered in 1645 by the Ottoman fleet. This is followed in 1647 by the capture of Réthimnon and 1648 sees the start of the siege of Candia (Iráklion) with whose fall in 1669 the Ottoman supremacy is complete. Crete receives another new administration with the division into legal districts (kazas), each ruled by a kadi. Many convert to Islam. In 1821 the Greek mainland rises up against the Ottomans and in 1822 proclaims Greece's independence. Not until 1898, however, do the Ottomans leave the island and Crete receives its independence under an allied high commissioner.

1898-1913, autonomous government: the prospect of joining with the motherland gains increasingly more popularity. In 1913 under Elefterios Venizelos, Crete achieves admission into the Greek state.

1913-1944, the world wars: Crete was not involved in the First World War. During the Second World War British troops are sent here from the mainland to keep Crete as a sea base for the British. The Germans land in 1941 and occupy the island until 1944. Many resistance fighters lose their lives.

1945 to the present day: after the war many family members have been forced to go abroad to work. Many villages are deserted, and even mainland industry attracts a Cretan workforce. The gradual rise in agricultural exports since entry into the EU in 1981 and a rapid increase in tourism have resulted in a now continuous upturn in prosperity on the island.

Information and addresses

Getting there
By air: for the majority of tourists, charter flights (March to October) are the cheapest means of travelling. Olympic Airways flies to Iraklion. There are also cheap charter flights to Athens, and from there you can take a plane or ferry to Crete.

By sea: boats daily from Piraeus (19.00) to Haniá and Iráklion and three times a week to Réthimnon. The crossing takes 11 hrs.

By car: from Italy there are ferries from Trieste, Ancona, Ortona, Brindisi, Bari and Otranto to Pátras, sometimes to Iráklion as well.

Information
Information on Crete is available from:
Great Britain: Greek National Tourist Organization, 4, Conduit Street, London W1R ODJ, tel: (0044171) 4994976, 7345997, Fax: 2871369;USA: Greek National Tourist Organization, Olympic Tower 645 Fifth Avenue – New York, NY 10022, tel: (001212) 4215777, Fax: 8266940

Camping
Although, as a rule, wild camping is not allowed in Greece, it's quite possible in Crete to put up a tent in the mountains or in isolated bays. However, there are police controls on the beaches of tourist resorts. There are about a dozen campsites on the island.

Theft
The times when you could leave your luggage unattended on the beach or elsewhere are gone. Break-ins are rare, but nevertheless, it's advisable not to leave anything valuable in your car.

Public holidays
1st January, 6th January, 25th March, Easter, 1st May, Whitsun, 15th August, 28th October, Christmas.

Climate

Iráklion's climate (average temperatures in °C)

Month	1	2	3	4	5	6	7	8	9	10	11	12	Year
Temperature ø °C	12	13	14	17	24	24	26	26	24	20	17	14	19
Maximum °C	16	16	17	20	24	28	29	29	27	24	21	17	22
Water °C	16	15	16	17	19	22	24	25	24	23	20	17	20

The sun shines on Crete 300 days in the year. What is more, the east is drier than the west. Spring is the most pleasant time for walking. The mild winter lasts three to four months and the coasts are always free of snow. Snow only falls in the mountains and stays until early summer in the highest places.

Emergency
There is no mountain rescue service in Crete. In case of emergency notify the nearest police station: police 100 – breakdown 104 – fire service 199.

Sport
Water sports and hiking are the most popular leisure pursuits. The tourist areas also offer surfing, sailing, diving, water skiing, and paragliding. You will find tennis courts in almost all the hotels and there's a growing number of mountain bike enthusiasts on Crete.

Telephone
The dialling code for Greece / Crete is 0030. The code from Crete to England is 0044.

Transport on Crete
Buses: the Cretan bus company KTEL maintains an extensive bus network on Crete. It is divided into KTEL Haniá / Réthimnon and KTEL Iráklion / Lassíthi and there's a current timetable available for each. A service runs to larger towns several times a day. There's a regular half-hourly to hourly service on the north coast highway between Agios Nikólaos in the east and Kastélli Kíssamou in the west. Buses run far less frequently in the winter.
Taxi: taxis operate with a meter in the towns, but in the country they are called Agoreon and there's a price list.
Hire car: on almost every street corner there are cars and motorbikes for rent. Cars are relatively expensive.

Boat services
Boats can play an important role for walkers on the south-western coast, but all the boat services are dependent on the weather and the time of year. Boats operate between Hóra Sfakíon, Loutró, Agia Rouméli, Soúgia and Paleohóra.

Time
In Greece the time is two hours ahead of England, so if it is 12.00 in England, it is 14.00 in Crete.

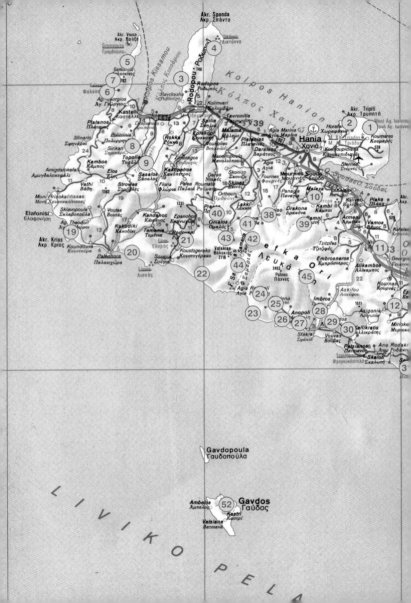

North-west Crete

The two highest mountain ranges on the island, the White Mountains and the Ida Mountains, shape the landscape in north-west Crete. Its north side might have plenty of water, but only a few coastal strips are important for their agricultural production. Cretan olive oil is some of the best in the world and countless olive trees constitute the main source of income for smallholders. While the cultivation of citrus fruits and vines plays only a subsidiary role in this part of the island, the breeding of sheep and goats is widespread.

Two towns form the economic centres of the region – the district capitals Haniá and Réthimnon. Both have quaint old-towns, narrow alleyways, and Venetian and Turkish houses grouped round the Venetian harbour. **Haniá**, the larger of the two, has about 60,000 inhabitants. The market hall is worth seeing, together with the Turkish mosque at the old harbour. A few kilometres south-east of Haniá is the port of Soúda. The big ferries dock here from Piraeus. **Soúda Bay** is one of the best-protected natural bays in the Mediterranean. It is no wonder, therefore, that there is a marine base situated here and the whole bay is a military safety zone. The Akrotíri peninsula is bursting with weapons, as it were, with a military airfield and a NATO training base, which stretches from Haniá and Soúda into the sea. The civil airport is situated here as well. It is worth paying a visit, whilst on this extensively developed peninsula, to the monasteries of Katholikó and Agia Triáda and there's a beautiful beach at Stavrós. Both the other peninsulas in the north-west, on the other hand, are inhabited by herds of sheep and goats. One of the special features of the **Rodopoú Peninsula** is the Diktynaion, a shrine dedicated to the goddess Diktyna, but only a few ruins are preserved. At the base of the peninsula is the Goniá monastery where the metropolitan district of Haniá, Irenaeus, has set up an academy for international economic studies. This district also organises big celebrations which take place every year on the 29th August at the Agios Ioánnis Giónis chapel on the peninsula. No less barren is the **Gramvoússa peninsula** in the far north-west which has a superb sandy bay called Tigáni Bálos. A Venetian fort, which did not surrender to the Turks until 1692, stands on the offshore island of the same name.

There is a string of sandy beaches if you drive along the road westwards from Haniá. Unfortunately the area around Agia Marína is over-developed with many hotels, rooms for rent, supermarkets, souvenir shops, and cars and mopeds for rent all along the road. After Kolimbári the road cuts through a hillside to reach the capital of the Kíssamos district, **Kastélli Kíssamou**. If you continue westwards you will come to the beautiful beach of **Falássarna** at the south-western corner of the Gramvoússa peninsula. The flat strip of coast and the ever-present sun provide ideal conditions for greenhouse cultivation. Falássarna and south of Kastélli, **Polirinía** are evidence of Dorian settlement in this part of the island. Those of you who are not put off by lengthy car or bus journeys should visit the wonderfully positioned **Hrissoskalítissas monastery** in the far south-west of the island and the delightful Elafoníssos islands. From the national highway on the north coast there are several, at times very winding roads, leading through the island's interior to the south coast. They go past numerous isolated villages with Byzantine churches from the middle-ages which are well worth a visit and provide an insight into rural life.

There's a whole series of **gorges** worth seeing in the north-west. There are roads through some of them so that you can easily experience them from the car, for example the Topolía gorge to the south of Kastélli or the Thérisso gorge to the south of Haniá, but the best impressions are gained by gorge walking.

The drive from Haniá to Réthimnon along the main highway takes barely an hour. **Georgioúpolis** lies between the two towns at the start of a kilometre-long stretch of sand. In the countryside to the south of the highway, surrounded by high mountains, is **Lake Kournás**, Crete's only lake.

The district capital **Réthimnon** has an enchanting Venetian harbour, and a Turkish and Venetian old quarter. The fortress overlooking the town is worth a visit. Réthimnon has about 20,000 inhabitants, but in the summer months the number of tourists exceeds that, with countless hotel complexes and rooms for rent beside the beaches east of Réthimnon. The coast does not become rocky and inaccessible until the slopes of the **Kouloúkonas mountains**. The countryside south of Réthimnon is mountainous too so that only a few roads go down to the south coast. The scenery as you drive down the **Kourtaliótiko** or **Kotsifoú gorge** to Plakiás is particularly impressive as is the drive through the **Amári basin**.

Citrus fruits at Georgioúpolis.

1 From Agia Triáda to Katholikó

To the Akrotíri monasteries

Agia Triáda – Gouvernéto – Arkoudhiótissa cave – Katholikó

Starting point: Agia Triáda monastery, 16km from Haniá.

This large peaceful monastery lies on the broad plain before the mountains of Akrotíri and is reached along a beautiful avenue of cypress trees. The grounds of the monastery are surrounded by a vast area of orange and olive groves and extensive vineyards.

Walking time: Agia Triáda – Gouvernéto 1 hr., Gouvernéto – the Bear's cave 20 mins., Bear's Cave – Katholikó 20 mins., Katholikó – coast 20 mins., return 2¼ hrs. Total time 4¼ hrs.

Difference in height: ascent 200m, descent 300m (one way).

Grade: easy gorge walk, mainly on good paths, short sections along the stony riverbed, a steep 5m descent, sturdy footwear necessary, little shade, possible all year round.

Stops and accommodation: several tavernas and cafés near to the airport. Hotels, rooms for rent and campsites in Haniá.

Bus services: twice daily, one on Sundays as far as Agia Triáda, several Olympic buses to the airport every day.

Tip: there's an entry fee of 1,17 Euros to the Agia Triáda monastery which is really worth a visit. Women must wear a long skirt and long sleeves. Closed 12.00-17.00.

A tarmac road goes north-west at first on level ground from **Agia Triáda**, later up 200m along a concrete road through a narrow valley to the **Gouvernéto** monastery. The fortress-like complex was built in 1548 under Venetian influence. The monastery is closed between 14.00 and 17.00 (entrance 1,47 Euros). From the nearby col there's a beautiful view northwards to the sea and a good footpath goes over an old road surface for 20 mins. down to some ruins and the Arkoudhiótissa cave, the **Bear's Cave**. An enormous stalagmite resembling a bear stands inside the cave. The chapel at the en-

The inner courtyard of the Agia Triáda monastery.

trance dates from the 14th century. After another 20 mins. down many steps into the gorge below, you reach a second cave. Each year on 7th October, the name day of the hermit Saint John, the cave becomes the meeting point for numerous pilgrims, some of whom spend the night here after evening mass.

The path goes down steep steps cut into the rock to the **Katholikó** monastery, situated a bit lower down. The monastery was partly destroyed after the invasion by Arabian pirates in the 16th century. Since then it has been uninhabitable and the monks moved into the higher Gouvernéto monastery. The monastery was built on a vast bridge arch which spans the gorge, at this point 15m wide, and cellars and cisterns are hidden in the walls. Follow the path across this archway and then immediately turn right and scramble down steeply for a few metres to the bottom of the gorge. Follow the dry stony riverbed for 20 mins. down to the sea and take in the wonderful scenery. On the **coast** there are still the ledges of an old quarry and an old boathouse made of stone.

High waves make the rocky coast unsuitable for swimming but you can get to swim in the narrow fjord-like bay from the old slipway.

Return the same way to the monasteries.

2 From Stavrós to the church of Agios Geórgios and to Katholikó

In the mountains of Akrotíri

Stavrós – Agios Geórgios – Katholikó monastery

Starting point: Stavrós, the northernmost town of the Akrotíri peninsula, once a beautiful small bathing resort but now lacking in character since the building development.

Walking time: Stavrós – Agios Geórgios 1¼ hrs., Agios Geórgios – col ½ hr., col – Katholikó monastery 1¾ hrs. Total time: Stavrós to Agios Geórgios and back 2½-3 hrs., Stavrós to Katholikó 3½ – 4 hrs.

Difference in height: 250m.

Grade: moderately difficult walk. Good route finding as far as the church, but after that it's more difficult, at times without paths or shade, only water from cisterns on the way.

Stops and accommodation: hotels, rooms for rent, holiday flats, restaurants, tavernas and bars in Haniá and Stavrós.

Bus services: three buses daily from Haniá in the tourist season.

Tip: a cave with a beautiful view on the steep mountainside above Stavrós, at a height of 250m.

Stavrós is well-known from the film 'Zorba the Greek' – the cable car which crashes dramatically to the ground and the marvellous dance scene on the beach were filmed here. This village was once so beautiful and peaceful with its delightful tiny lagoon, and is now hopelessly overrun.

Just before the road reaches the beach it turns off right before the last houses to the edge of the lagoon and runs along beside it towards the hill east of the village. This is where you will see the afore-mentioned cave. After the

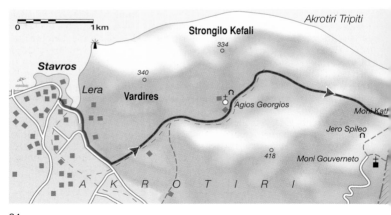

last fenced-off pasture a footpath crosses to the south. Follow this until it ends a few minutes later at a newly extended road. This road leads eastwards to the start of the gorge and you follow it right to the end (20 mins. from Stavrós).

Taking a distinct footpath past an old cistern, continue through the still flat valley along the dry riverbed. At times on the right of the stream but mainly in the valley bottom, the path becomes increasingly narrow and then goes gradually uphill between the steepening hills. There are occasional cairns as waymarkers. About half an hour from the start of the footpath go up the left-hand side of the valley just above the little gorge and then back down the few metres into the stony riverbed which you follow for another 10 mins. The valley begins to level out and forks at the point where there are some ruins up on the left and a large intact water cistern. Go up the hillside here to the ruins and only just before you reach them you will see the **Agios Geórgios** church and the nearby cave hidden behind carob and oak trees. The church is built directly into the entrance of the cave and from its forecourt there's a beautiful view down into the valley. There are ruins everywhere which suggest the former site of a large monastery.

You need a good sense of direction for the next stage of the walk as the hills all look alike. Go from the church across the hillside back to the streambed which you follow until it ends at a large carob tree after about 100m. Follow the reddish tracks and keeping along the line of the valley, go uphill towards a high col. Going past another large cistern with several watering troughs you will find the occasional cairn and after half an hour from the church you are standing on the **col**, 300m, with an open view across to the north-east and the sea.

The next part of your walk goes down into the valley below and then again follow the reddish soil going eastwards through the valley. This high valley widens out into a plain and you cross the length of it to the east. There's a small descending valley at the end of the plain, 45 mins. from the col to this point. The valley floor is densely overgrown at the start. Under fairly large trees you come into the small, increasingly deep ravine. As it gets narrower more and more rock formations appear on both sides and the valley is transformed into a steep gorge. Most of the time you can walk along the streambed and it's only necessary in a few places to clamber down rocky steps.

At a fork in the gorge go left and after a further 45 mins. from the high plain you come suddenly, after a bend, to a small basin-shaped valley. This is where the **Katholikó** monastery was built on top of an enormous archway. Following a good footpath go up from here to the monasteries of **Gouvernéto** and **Agia Triáda** (see Walk 1).

3   From Rodopós to Agios Ioánnis Giónis

Barren peninsula with isolated church and beautiful coastal path

Rodopós – Agios Ioánnis – Rodopós

Starting point: village square in Rodopós, about 7.2km from Kolimbári.
Walking time: Rodopós – Agios Ioánnis Giónis 2¼ hrs, return along the coast 2¾ hrs. Total time 5 hrs.
Difference in height: 580m.
Grade: requiring stamina, but not a difficult walk.

Good footwear. Water.
Stops and accommodation: restaurants and hotels in Kolimbári, kafenía in Rodopós.
Bus services: twice daily from Haniá to Rodopós.
Tip: the walk goes partly along a gravel road that is regularly used.

Each year on the 29th August, thousands of people make a pilgrimage to the remote site of Agios Ioánnis Giónis and then there's a festival lasting for more than several days, with masses and a multi-baptising of children and newborn babies organised by the metropolitan borough of Kíssamos. Afterwards this oasis in a barren landscape is once more shrouded in isolation.

The starting point for the walk is the cathedral square in **Rodopós**. At a statue take the road which leaves the village past a blue and white church. After a good kilometre you can take a shortcut at a left-hand bend. Then it continues along the gravel road climbing slowly upwards. After ¾ hr. you pass two concrete pillars (the one on the right has tipped over). About 1½ hrs. from the start of the walk you will see a **signpost** (pros Agios Ioánnis) at a fork in the road next to a water cistern. This is for cars.

Go left here past the cistern along the broad gravel path and in 10 mins. you will be standing on a pass. As you descend you will soon come past a **light blue roadway shrine**. From here you have a marvellous view down onto the little church surrounded by a square of open grazing land and across to the Gramvoússa peninsula with the offshore islands. Notice too the curious model church shrine on the path. After a good 2 hrs. you reach the site of the churches (**Agios Ioánnis** and **Agios Nikólaos**). A round font and long rows of stone tables under shady trees come into view. An agreeable place to take a rest.

The next stage of your walk begins at the gateway to the church along the path going southwards (faintly marked orange). Keeping straight ahead and past a broken wire fence, walk on to a sheep pen. In the distance you will soon see the town of Kastélli. Cross over a gorge which goes down to the sea. You will see the **Agios Pávlos** chapel at the bottom. There's a short gentle descent until the path goes up again and swings left away from the coast.

Continuing on a gravel road again and left at a fork, keep straight on until you can see **Rodopós**. Look out for a shortcut right (past a playing field) and then rejoin the roadway which brings you into the village.

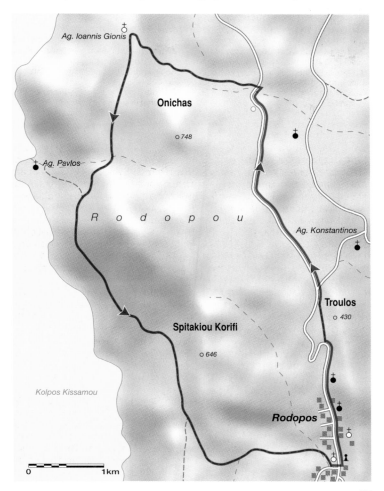

4 To the temple of Diktyna on the Rodopoú peninsula

Rocky bay and stumps of antique pillars at the end of a barren peninsula

Rodopós – temple of Diktyna – Rodopós

Starting point: drive along the road which leads from Rodopós (7.2km from Kolimbári) out onto the peninsula for 6.3km as far as the water cisterns and signpost (see walk 3) or further.
Walking time: cisterns – wide right-hand bend 1½ hrs., bend – Diktyna bay 1½ hrs. Total time 6 hrs. including return.
Difference in height: 500m.

Grade: easy, but lengthy walk without any shade. Needs stamina.
Stops and accommodation: restaurants and hotels in Kolimbári, kafenía in Rodopós.
Connections: best to take a car to the starting point.
N.B.: the walk goes along a regularly used gravel road.

It is best to do the first section of this route by car as walking there and back would be far too long. The reward of this walk is the beautiful bay with the stone ruins of the former Diktyna temple on a terrace above the southern

The bay where the temple of the love-shy Diktyna once stood.

edge. This is where the love-shy nymph Diktyna is supposed to have plunged into the water to escape the advances of the lecherous Minos. The fishermens' nets saved her and gave her her name (dichti = net).

The first 6.3km are identical to Walk 3. This section is well maintained and can be driven by car. So begin the walk at the **water cisterns with the signpost** marked 'pros Agios Ioánnis'. After 600m there's another sign to the left, but it's straight on to the shrine. Keep following the main path. After ¾ hr. you come past another cistern and then the path keeps going downwards. After you have passed some deserted quarries the road curves broadly round to the right. You can take a shortcut if you like. You will come to a sheep farm after 2 hrs. and then start to descend almost in the opposite direction. Finally the path goes eastwards through a gorge to the bay. This is the most beautiful part of the walk. On the right above the bay, called Ménies, are the ruins of the former **Diktyna temple**. The ruins on the other side of the bay are probably of Turkish origin. On the way back you can take a brisk shortcut up a steep mule track (15 minutes).

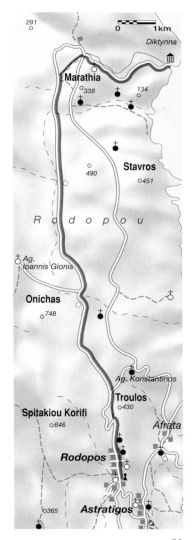

5   To the pirates' bay 'Tigáni Bálos'

From the gulf of Kastélli across the Gramvoússa peninsula

Kalivianí – Agia Iríni – Tigáni Bálos

The bay of Tigáni Bálos: turquoise water and fine coral sand.

Starting point: Kalivianí, 7km from Kastélli, the capital of the district of Kíssamos on the gulf of Kastélli, situated between the peninsulas of Gramvoússa and Rodopoú.
Park at the end of the gravel road (coming from Kalivianí).
Walking time: descent 30 mins., ascent 40 mins.
Difference in height: 150m.

Grade: easy walk.
Stops and accommodation: taverna and 2 hotels in Kalivianí, tavernas and kafenía in Kastélli.
Bus services: three times daily Kastélli – Plátanos, bus stop 1km before Kalivianí at a crossroads.
Tip: in summer there's a daily boat service from Haniá and Tráhilos (west of Kastélli) to Gramvoússa.

This walk takes you to the north-west corner of Crete, the bay of pirates 'Tigáni Bálos'. It begins in the small village of **Kalivianí**, going northwards along a gravel road directly past the church. The gravel road goes up the east side of the peninsula to the north, past a stranded old freighter, with marvellous views of the gulf of Kastélli and the Rodopoú peninsula on the opposite side of the bay. Go past the **Agia Iríni chapel** where there's a vigorously bubbling spring right beside it – a good opportunity to take a break. Along the gravel road which crosses over the flat ridge there's a breathtaking view of the west side of Gramvoússa. Below you can see **Tigáni**

Bálos bay, the name of which means something like 'frying pan' and is quite clearly related to the shape of this shallow lagoon.

The two islands of Agria Gramvóussa and Imeri Gramvóussa lie to the north-west – 'the wild and the gentle' – with turquoise-coloured water and white sand. There are the ruins of a Venetian fortress still to be seen on Imeri Gramvoússa which, as Crete's last stronghold, was able to withstand the Turks until it finally surrendered in 1692.

In about 30 mins. from the car park at the end of the gravel road you reach the bay below. The somewhat steep descent is flanked on the left by a huge mountain, the Mávros Póros. The shallow lagoon with its white dunes, the finest coral sand and its infinite spectrum of blue tones caused by the varying depths of the water and the two offshore islands, is one of Crete's most beautiful bays. But unfortunately even here pollution is on the increase. Not only an amazing amount of tar on the beaches ruins the landscape, but also the rubbish carelessly left behind mainly by tourists who come here by boat.

There are two huts on the beach which provide a kiosk and bar in the summer. If you have enough time you can wade through the water (mainly over sharp volcanic rock) to Cape Tigáni where a **chapel** has been erected on the highest point.

6 To the ruins of the port of Falássarna

Over the mountain ridge down to the white sands of Falássarna

Kalivianí – Azogirás – Falássarna

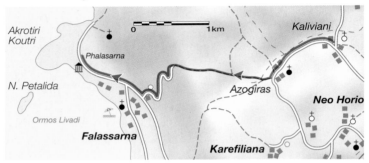

Starting point: Kalivianí, 7km from Kastélli, 1km from the road between Kastélli and Plátanos.
Walking time: Kalivianí – Azogirás ½ hr., Azogirás – top of the pass ½ hr., pass – tavernas 1 hr., tavernas – Falássarna ½ hr. Total time 2½ hrs.
Difference in height: ascent 150m, descent 200m.
Grade: easy walk across a high ridge, mainly on field paths. Very hot in summer.

Stops and accommodation: rooms and tavernas in Falássarna.
Bus services: Kastélli – Falássarna 10.00, 17.00. Kastélli – Plátanos three times a day.
Boat services: boat service in summer from Tráhilos (west of Kastélli) to Falássarna.
Tip: ancient port in Falássarna and in Polirinía, the first Dorian settlement in Crete.

Leave the village of Kalivianí to the north-west on a broad field path which soon becomes a track. Go uphill gradually at first and right along the now broad path and then at the fork you descend left. Once you reach the gravel road you turn off right and come to the houses of **Azogirás**. In the village, roads branch off in all directions and you keep to the left continuing past the individual houses (take no notice of the red arrow pointing to the left at the last ruin) as the road starts to deteriorate. Go through a gate, then left and turn immediately right after another gate and keep walking uphill in front of the olive grove.

From here the path to the **pass** is well-marked. From the ridge there's a glorious view over the plain below where the greenhouses are glinting in the sun backed by the sea. It will take just under an hour to descend the winding gravel road (at a height of 200m) to reach the tavernas on the coast. Below

Probably an old quarry close to ancient Falássarna.

the taverna, which stands on an incline, there's a vigorous spring coming from a rock. It provides water for the new village of Falássarna and is also used by the many campers who live on the beach. The route now follows a gravel road for half an hour and goes past greenhouses and through orange groves to the old port of **Falássarna**. This town dates from the 4th and 5th centuries B.C. and under the Dorians was at its high point as the second port of Polirinía. It was supposedly destroyed in the big earthquake in the 5th century B.C. Many ruins are still to be found, including a large stone throne, stone chambers, and tombs, and in the actual old town area which was concentrated on the hill further north, there are the ruins of a retaining wall and the old acropolis.

You need to plan a good 3 hrs. for the return, but this vast beach is certainly a tempting place to stay longer (in which case you should ring ahead to book a room).

7 From Falássarna to Gramvoússa

Along the wild north-west coast of Crete

Falássarna – Geróskinos – Gramvoússa

Starting point: Falássarna, in the extreme north-west of the island. The 5km tarmac road from Plátanos ends by the last tavernas above the long beautiful beach of Falássarna.

Walking time: tavernas – end of the road ½ hr., ascent to the terrace ½ hr., start of the terrace – rocky bay 1½ hrs, ascent to the rock face (Geróskinos) ¾ hr., traversing below the rock faces 1½ hrs., descent to the lagoon of Gramvoússa ½ hr. Total time 5½ hrs.

Difference in height: 500m.

Grade: difficult and strenuous coastal walk demanding sure-footedness, fitness and good route-finding ability. Hardly any shade, no drinking water on the route, 3 hrs. needed for the return to Kalivianí. Sturdy footwear!

Stops and accommodation: tavernas and rooms in Falássarna, 2 hotels in Kalivianí, hotels, rooms and campsite in Kastélli.

Bus services: Kastélli – Falássarna 10.00, 17.00, Kastélli – Plátanos three times a day.

Boat services: in summer there's a boat service from Tráhilos (west of Kastélli) to Falássarna.

Tip: ruins of the old port of Falássarna directly by the sea, also ruins of a settlement on the steep hill to the north of the old town.

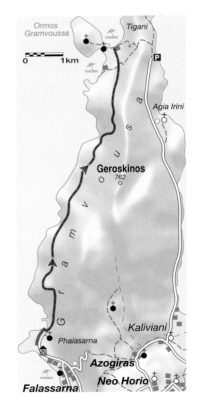

One of the last tavernas in **Falássarna** stands on an incline with a vigorous spring coming from a rock. At these tavernas take the gravel road past greenhouses and through olive groves to the old town 1km away. Foundations and derelict buildings, an old throne and sarcophagus are the evidence of this once large and thriving port.

The **road ends** at a pasture fence. After the gate a narrow footpath leads up onto the hill in the north and after half an hour reaches a 200m high **terrace** which falls away steeply down left to the sea. A narrow, but mainly visible path with cairns goes over fairly level ground northwards at a height of about 150 to 200m. After a short descent your route goes across a deep valley, about 250m wide, and ascends on the opposite side again close to the **yellowish rocks**.

In the process the narrow path ends at a small goat shed built right under the rocks. Go through it to get to the top of the rocks on the other side of this valley. Take note of this spot for your eventual return. Continue on gently sloping ground with an open view down to the steep coastline and the sea, the narrow path descends between boulders till it comes to a small **rocky bay** (2½ hrs.). The path, up to this point, is mainly used by shepherds. You now see in front of you a wild and inaccessible strip of coast. Steep rock and scree slopes, interspersed with ravines and ridges from the almost 800m high **Geróskinos**, drop down to the sea. There's no way through to the coast, but from the bay there's a steep gully going up to the start of the rock faces. Climb up small goat paths across a steep hillside to the right of it until, in ¾ hr., you are directly under the **rock face**. Here, at a height of about 200m just under the rock faces, there's an obvious footpath going northwards, at times over boulders and through dense undergrowth. You have to go round the bottom of the ridges as they drop down to the coast but the path still continues to go along close to the **rock faces**. As you cross the scree slopes you need to be able to read the terrain well. There are only occasional cairns and it's possible to lose your way. After a traverse of about 1½ hrs. a steep boulder field leads up into a **narrow cleft** where there's a large cairn. Go through and down across the upper edge of a broad rocky gully. Keeping to the right hand side, close to the rocks, the path goes diagonally downwards, crosses round the top of a steep gully and reaches an open hillside. Ahead is the lagoon of **Gramvoússa**.

The constant searching for the right path, having to take care over difficult terrain and the climbing over rocks and scree is now over. In contrast, the path continues down through sand dunes and undergrowth to the white coral sand and the pale blue and turquoise water. Unfortunately this idyllic picture is spoilt by all the rubbish and lumps of tar on the beach. Drinks are on sale at two small bars here in the summer for the tourists, who come mainly by boat. Return as in Walk 5.

8 From Sirikári to Polirinía

Through the Tsikhlianá gorge to the Dorian fortress

Sirikári – Tsikhlianá gorge – Polirinía

Starting point: Sirikári, 19km south of Ka-stélli.
Walking time: Sirikári – start of the gorge ¾ hr., gorge 1 hr., end of the gorge – Poli-rinía ¾ hr., ascent of the hill at Polirinía ½ hr. Total time 2½ – 3 hrs.
Difference in height: ascent 220m, des-cent 330m.
Grade: easy mountain walk.
Stops and accommodation: restaurants and hotels in Kastélli. Taverna in Polirinía. Kafeníon in Sirikári.
Bus services: Kastélli – Sirikári twice weekly, Kastélli – Polirinía twice daily.

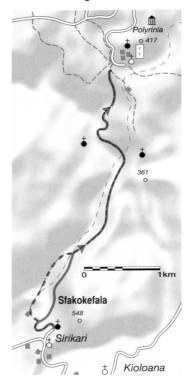

Despite the fact that the starting point is difficult to reach by public transport this walk is one of the most rewarding in western Crete. It combines an impressive gorge walk with a classically beautiful panoramic view from the hill of the Dorian mountain village of Polirinía. The walk begins in the small moun-tain village of **Sirikári**. From the end of the village walk to the church about 10 mins. away. The path down into the gorge begins oppo-site the church door. Go through a fence and descend an easy re-cognisable path across terraces. Through another fence, the path crosses over a broader path and then sub-divides. Go right here fol-lowing an old paved path, maintai-ning height across the slope until you come to an abandoned village (4-5 houses).
Alternative: go left here towards the buildings opposite. Through yet another fence the path brings you down to the stream. On the other side climb up high to some solitary houses and go past the lowest one to the right and continue parallel to

View from a cave on the way up the Tsikhlianá gorge.

the streambed down into the gorge. After passing through a gate you experience your first view of the dramatic scenery of the **Tsikhlianá gorge**. Cross over to the other side of the stream at a ramshackle bridge.

The comfortable path begins to ascend gently after 1½ hours and reaches the streambed again at a cobbled **arch bridge**. Cross the bridge and you will see the houses of **Polirinía** in the distance. Through a fence and then past a water pipe you come to a roadway which brings you up to the village. There's a taverna with a beautiful terrace by the spring at the edge of the village. This is a good place to take a rest before climbing up the hill above the village. From the taverna, walk into the village as far as a small kafeníon. Climb up the steep steps on the left to the cemetery. This is where the path begins to wind up right round the hill.

Go past some ruins and in half an hour you can be enjoying a magnificent panorama from the summit.

9   Round the top of the Topóliá gorge

In the mountains behind Kastélli

Katsamatádos – Mourí – Voulgáro

Starting point: Katsamatádos or Topóliá (about 12km from Kastélli).
Walking time: Topóliá gorge ½ hr., Katsamatádos – pass 1 hr., pass – Mourí 1½ hrs., Mourí – Voulgáro 1 hr. Total time 3½-4 hrs.
Difference in height: ascent 270m, descent 450m.

Grade: not difficult for the most part, but there's a moderately difficult section with a short climb in a gorge (½ hr).
Stops and accommodation: restaurants and hotels in Kastélli, tavernas in Katsamatádos and Voulgáro, kafeníon in Mourí.
Bus services: Kastélli – Topóliá twice daily.

The actual starting point of the walk is Katsamatádos. The drive through the Topóliá gorge is so impressive that if you want to experience the breathtaking scenery to the full you should leave the bus in Topóliá and go on foot along the road through the gorge (½ hr.). 1.9km after Topóliá and 400m before the place-name sign of Katsamatádos there's a climb up to the **Agia Sophía cave** (10 mins.) which is not to be missed. A tiny church has been built into this cave with stalagmites and stalactites and from here there's a splendid view of the gorge.

A path goes up to the Agia Sophía cave just before Katsamatádos.

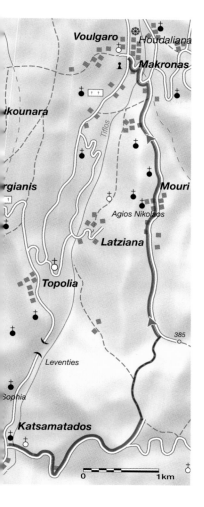

300m behind the southern place-name sign of **Katsamatádos** a concrete path leads over a bridge into the village. Go past the kafeníon and straight ahead into the side valley, keeping the stream on the left. Go through a cattle gate and continue upwards. After 25 mins. the roadway swings round to the left, past a stone hut and wooden feeding troughs and through a fence. As you ascend the gravel road you can look back and see the houses of Katsamatádos.

After an hour you pass through a gate on the top of the **pass**. Turn left onto the roadway a few metres below you (the right fork goes to Sásalos). After 8 minutes the path leads north into a cleft of a valley where there are vineyards on the left. A few minutes later climb over a wire fence to reach the tiny church of **Agios Athanásios**. Follow the path along the line of the deeply incised streambed or directly in it if the going gets too difficult. After about 20 mins. in the **gorge** you will see a pipeline running along the left wall. You have to use your hands at times on the descent. It's not much further after the cattle gate until you come to a roadway. Go to the left and follow it to Mourí.

After 2 hrs. 20 mins. you reach the houses of **Mourí**. On a little-used tarmac road leave the village and you will reach **Voulgáro** in just under an hour.

10 From Katohóri to Stílos

Through the Díktamos gorge

Katohóri – Díktamos gorge – Stílos

Starting point: Katohóri, 300m. The village lies just below the road from Kondopoúla to Kámbi, in the bottom of a fertile valley in the northern foothills of the White Mountains, 20km away from Haniá.
Walking time: bus stop – village square 20 mins., village square – end of the gorge 2½ hrs., end of the gorge – road Stílos 20 mins. Total time 3 hrs. 10 mins.
Difference in height: 250m.
Grade: easy gorge walk, although without paths, sturdy footwear necessary, some sections likely to be wet, predominantly shady, not possible after heavy rainfall.

Stops and accommodation: kafenía and tavernas in Stílos and Néo Horió, hotels and campsite in Haniá.
Bus services: Haniá – Kámbi 6.00. Stílos – Haniá 11.15, 16.20, 17.30, at weekends 11.15, 16.20, 18.30. The times change from winter to summer (not contained in the timetable). Because of infrequent service from Katohóri it is advisable to do the walk in the given direction.
Tip: high above Soúda bay there's the old town of Aptera, and a Byzantine church shortly before Stílos as well as ruins of a Minoan town.

This walk is ideal either in spring, with the luxuriant display of blossoms (particularly at the start) or in late autumn with the leaves changing colour, or even in the hotter months as a welcome addition to a beach holiday. You are recommended to take the early morning bus from Haniá. On its way from Maláxa the bus stops in front of a small bridge. Continue on foot, straight ahead for a while (sign: *Haniá 21km*), until you come to a concrete

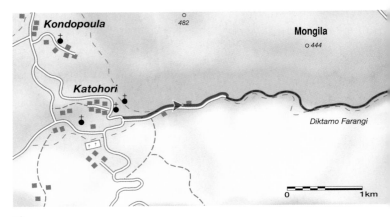

road on a sharp bend, which takes you past a small chapel to the village of **Katohóri**. The kafeníon in the village square, shaded by tall plane trees, usually seems to be shut. Past the kafeníon on the right hand side the path goes northwards towards an imposing rock projection. Following a footpath you walk past orchards and orange groves, descending gently towards the gorge which is already visible. In between isolated groups of trees in this sweeping landscape you have an open view south-eastwards towards the first summits of the White Mountains.

Start by following a running stream, crossing from side to side. You need to circumnavigate certain places where the water is too deep, but always follow the blue arrows. The stream dries up in the gorge, but it is evident from eroded rock formations and polished tree stumps that some water does flow through here, especially in spring and after heavy rainfall. After about an hour the gorge widens for a while into a large hollow and you are able to see more clearly the fantastic landscape. Having walked for almost 3 hrs., nearly always in shade, the **gorge** eventually **broadens out** and there is flat ground ahead. Following the blue waymarkers go up right, out of the streambed, onto the parallel running roadway. Only a few minutes at a fork later you cross the streambed again and come to some houses left above the stream. Go past them on the right onto a concrete roadway, bringing you in another 10 mins. to the road to **Stílos** and then another 10 minutes to the village itself.

Water is plentiful in Stílos. The abundant springs are used by small drinks firms and the giant plane trees with their pleasant shade benefit from the rich supply of water. Directly in the square there's a taverna where you can take a comfortable break while you wait for the next bus. Buses travel back to Haniá from the village of Néo Horió as well, only 20 mins. away.

If you have your own car it is recommended that you begin the walk from Stílos. Leave the car at the **old bridge** just before Stílos and walk as far as you want up the gorge. The walk takes a maximum of 6 hrs., including return.

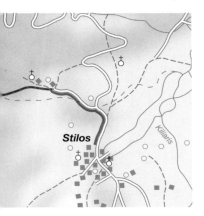

11 From Georgioúpolis to Likotinereá

To the villages in Apokóronou

Georgioúpolis – Argiromoúri – Likotinereá – Sellía – Georgioúpolis

Starting point: Georgioúpolis, beach resort on the north coast between Haniá and Réthimnon, the longest continuous beach on Crete's north coast.

Walking time: Georgioúpolis – Argiromoúri ¾ hr., Argiromoúri – Likotinereá 1½ hrs., Likotinereá – Sellía – Exópolis 2 hrs., Exópolis – Georgioúpolis 1½ hrs. Total time 5 hrs.

Difference in height: 350m.

Grade: easy walk, more than half of the route goes along tarmac or gravel roads.

Stops and accommodation: all types of rooms in Georgioúpolis, rooms in Exópolis, tavernas and kafenía in all villages.

Bus services: Georgioúpolis is on the main bus route between Haniá and Réthimnon with an hourly service.

Georgioúpolis has gradually become quite a substantial beach resort due to its location on the longest beach on the north coast and its proximity to the National highway. The amount of new building and the number of tavernas, bars and boutiques have increased accordingly. The village square with its high eucalyptus trees is a big attraction for the tourists. If you want to escape the hustle and bustle for a day you should visit the nearby villages in the district of Apokóronou and on this walk you can enjoy the tranquillity of less spectacular but delightful scenery.

Leave **Georgioúpolis** to the north, go past the harbour and over the new bridge. At first the road winds up 130m through luxuriant gardens

Agaves with their unusual flowers below Argiromoúri.

and fruit orchards into the old village of Argiromoúri, close to Exópolis. You can avoid the hairpin bends by taking a shortcut along a footpath that ends up at the tavernas of **Agiromoúri**. On the first big bend after the turn-off to the disco, a narrow field path turns off right and meets the tarmac road again 10 mins. later. The panorama taverna lies on the right at the top of the incline at a crossroads.

Directly next to the Georgia taverna a sign indicates the way to Likotinereá going through the orchards and then up the steeper hill. Following the blue and red waymarkers the path climbs up to the 300m hill on a wide bend. At times you can see the ruins of a former wide connecting route (road surfaces and supporting walls) and the path is easy to find, but at other times it is overgrown and hidden.

Several villages appear as you look around the undulating landscape and soon the first orchards point to the village of **Likotinereá** close by. Just before, the footpath finishes on a newly extended road which you leave after

Springtime amongst the ruins of Argiromoúri. Kástro in the background.

300m by descending on the old path again. Walk under olive trees and past beautiful orchards until you reach the village road. Go right and follow this to the end where a wonderful **viewing terrace** invites you to take a break. After an hour and a half's walking you can enjoy the splendid view down over the coast and along towards the sea of houses at Réthimnon.

For the return, first walk along the road and through the village to the road from Kefalá to Sellía where you'll find the only taverna and then continue left in the direction of Sellía. After 10 mins., opposite the last single house (with a wall around it) there's an old but well-maintained path which leads up to the somewhat higher cemetery and a chapel (there's a short stretch of concrete a bit later on). From here there's a beautiful view of Likotinereá.

You can continue along the old path past the church for 10 mins. up to the highest point, 400m, and enjoy from there the wonderful panorama across the whole region. From the church it's a few metres along the concrete access road down to the connecting road and into **Sellía**. At the end of the village at the fork a newly tarmac road winds 250m down towards Exópolis. After the fourth hairpin (at the end of a longish straight section) descend left at the narrow bend, following the still maintained old footpath down left to the road between Vámos and Georgioúpolis or continue down the tarmac road. At the turn-off go southwards until you reach the village of **Exópolis** in 1km. The quickest way to return to Georgioúpolis is to go right at the beginning of the village down onto the road below.

However it's far nicer to go left past the church (a beautiful viewing terrace), through the village which runs along the edge of the hillside and back to the tavernas in **Argiromoúri**. From here it's half an hour back to your starting point.

The small sheltered harbour of Georgioúpolis on the Almirós river.

12 From Argiroúpolis to Agios Philosías and Agios Elías

Walk in the hinterland of Réthimnon

Argiroúpolis – Agios Philosías – Agios Elías

Starting point: Argiroúpolis, on the western border of the district of Réthimnon, 6km south of Episkopí on a steep hill and built on the ruins of the ancient town of Lappa.

Walking time: Argiroúpolis – Agios Philosías 1 hr., A. Philosías – turn-off A. Elías 50 mins., turn-off – A. Elías 20 mins., A. Elías – Argiroúpolis ½ hr. Total time 3 hrs.

Difference in height: 200m.

Grade: easy walk on good paths (mostly narrow concrete or gravel side roads), lots of shade and an area with plenty of water.

Stops and accommodation: rooms and tavernas in Argiroúpolis and Episkopí, bed and breakfast and hotels all along the north coast between Réthimnon and Georgioúpolis.

Bus services: the old road from Réthimnon via Episkopí to Georgioúpolis, twice a day, Episkopí – Argiroúpolis – Asi Goniá once a day.

Tip: particularly worth seeing is the lower part of the picturesque village of Argiroúpolis, a large mountain village built on the ruins of the old town of Lappa. It lies in a densely wooded area in the eastern foothills of the White Mountains just before the steep barren hills drop down to the fertile plain on the north coast.

The walk begins in the church square up in the village of **Argiroúpolis** at a height of 300m, going through unspectacular but pleasant and peaceful countryside. Directly behind the church a narrow road brings you down into the lower village. Through narrow alleyways, past churches and old houses dating from different architectural eras, you leave the village towards the south.

The roadway runs along the densely wooded hillside from where there's a view deep into the valley and across to the mountains opposite. A few minutes after the village, keep left uphill at a turn off and along this roadway you reach a gravel road coming from the left above (from the road between Argiroúpolis and Miriokefala) and follow this to the right. It leads to **Philosías**

The lower part of Argiroúpolis. The little church of Agios Elías in the background.

church 1km away. Shortly before the church your route goes up left at another turn-off. The little church lies in a green well-irrigated oasis – a cool, tranquil and agreeably shady place. Go back down the same path till you are close to the village but then continue left along the first broad path to the cemetery with the **Elías church** on a small hill. It is 20 mins. from the first turn-off to the church. It stands on the hill which drops down steeply into the valley and gives you a beautiful view back to **Argiroúpolis** and into the deep mountain valley below. You will need another half an hour to return to Argiroúpolis.

Before returning it's worth visiting the upper part of the village as well. Go through the archway and then up to the ruins of the old town. Narrow alleys, beautiful inner courtyards and a view down onto the rooftops of the lower village and out towards the Cretan north coast are the highlights.

13 Along the E4 through the Poros gorge

Walk via Agios Konstantínos to Velonádo and Káto Póros

Agios Konstantínos – Velonádo – Káto Póros – Agios Konstantínos

Starting point: Agios Konstantínos.
Walking times: Agios Konstantínos – Velonádo 2¼ hrs., Velonádo – Káto Póros 1¾ hrs., Káto Póros – Agios Konstantínos ¾ hr. Total time 4¾ hrs.
Difference in height: 400m.
Grade: a sense of direction necessary as the waymarkings are poor in places.
Stops and accommodation: hotels and rooms for rent in Georgioúpolis or Réthimnon.

In **Agios Konstantínos** beside the well and a chapel next to house no. 153 there's a concrete path leading downhill by a dry-stone wall. Ignore two turn-offs to the left. Turn off left at an E4 sign by a mulberry tree and also at the next fork follow the E4 sign to the left. The path leads in between laurel and myrtle bushes and immediately continues as a narrow stony path down into a gorge which you cross. A path runs uphill on the other side between dry-stone walls.
Follow the black and yellow waymarkings until you cross a farm track going steeply uphill again between dry-stone walls. At another track you come to a chapel. Along the track on the left past the ruins of an abandoned village you keep going uphill almost to the highest point. Before a left-hand bend, continue straight on across limestone terrain.
Waymarkings indicate the path straight ahead onto the slope and

Transport: it's the best to drive there by car.

Narrow rock faces mark the most beautiful point of the Poros gorge.

over the rounded mountain top after which you can see the houses of
Velonádo.
Now descend along marked stony paths to the asphalt road. Follow this
slightly uphill to the right until after about 20 minutes at a waymarker pole a
field path leads into a streambed. Continue walking along this through the
impressive gorge. As soon as the gorge widens out again the waymarkings
leave the streambed up to the left where you go uphill along a track. This
meets another track: go left here and after 6m turn right onto a narrow path
which ends in **Káto Póros**.
Keeping right as you leave the village and return along the road (4.1km) via
Zourídi to **Agios Konstantínos**.

14 To Bonripári fortress

From Monopári to the Venetian Turkish fortifications of Bonripári

Monopári – Bonripári

Starting point: Monopári, 350m, a small village in the hinterland of Réthimnon, on the approach road to Káto Maláki, about 10km away from Goniá and situated on the old road.

Walking time: end of the village – foot of the fortress ¾ hr., ascent and walk round ½ hr., return ¾ hr. Total time 2 hrs.

Differnce in height: 200m.

Grade: easy walk, little shade, good route finding.

Stops and accommodation: kafeniá and tavernas in the villages along the approach road, rooms of all kinds close to Réthimnon.

Bus services: Réthimnon – Maláki 6.00 weekdays (except in the school holidays) and returns about 16.00.

There is hardly a more suitable site for a fortress in Crete than the fortified mound of Bonripári from where there's a fantastic panoramic view. It lies in the middle of a 180 degree loop of a gorge which the river Pétres flows through in its upper course between the villages of Monopári and Káto Maláki. Vertical walls over 100m high form the border to the plateau and its fortress can only be reached from the north via a hollow. In order to close off, so to speak, this amazing place, the Venetians built the fortification and it was used again under Turkish occupation.

Go past **Monopári** church and at the end of the village head for Káto Maláki. The road leaves the village on a bend to the south where there's a roadway turning off left leading to some sheds. After about 150m, just before some large newly-built cisterns, there's an old footpath with worn flagstones and border walls on the left at a large carob tree. Walking up here is like going into another age. At first the path goes under the shade of large olive and carob trees, then past rocks and along the hill with a view over the fortifications. After crossing the stream in a small side valley the path divides. Ascend left for a while and walk mostly on open ground towards the hollow in front of the fortress. Running up from the **hollow** to the site ruins there's a ridge of ground with a path. Go past an old tower and up a short steep section to reach the plateau. There's an impressive view on all sides from the

*View from the fortress of Bonripári over the Pétres river gorge towards
the White Mountains.*

Cretan Sea in the north, across the mountains in the east and the south and
to the start of the White Mountains in the west. You can walk round the plateau on the edge of the precipice looking down more than 100m into the
gorge as it winds round the fortifications of **Bonripári**. Return to Monopári
on the same path. You can, if you want, take a trip into the gorge itself. Drive
down the road into the narrow valley and walk through the gorge along tiny
overgrown goat paths. A path begins at the bridge and goes mainly up the
right-hand side of the valley just above the stream, but it's rather difficult to
find it. The valley bottom is totally overgrown. You can avoid sections of
deep water and an impassable narrow ravine in the upper part by going up
the steep slope.

15 Prassanó gorge

Between smoothly polished rocks and oleander bushes to the sea

Mírthios – Prassanó gorge – Missíria

Starting point: road junction Prassiés / Mírthios, about 26km from Réthimnon.
Walking time: junction – start of the gorge 1 hr., walk through the gorge 3 hrs., end of the gorge – Missíria 1½ hrs. Total time 5½ hrs.
Difference in height: 215m.

Grade: easy gorge walk along a dry streambed (from the middle of June). Take a second pair of shoes with you incase there is water in the pools.
Stops and accommodation: restaurants and hotels in Réthimnon.
Bus services: Réthimnon – Amári one to two buses a day.

Although the walk is not difficult you still need rather an adventurous spirit to 'fight' your way through the narrow riverbed. Next to the Tsiríta gorge this is one of the most beautiful in the Réthimnon area. It's especially interesting in spring when the pools are still full of water and your only means of getting through is to climb round or else wade through the water. But this is in June at the latest. The stream has dried up by then and only the pale colourings of the boulders are evidence of the height of the water at other times.

The walk starts at the **turn-off to Mírthios**, best reached by bus from Réthimnon to Amári. Ask the driver to let you off here. Follow the road for about 500m then take the concrete road down left. You can see the gorge quite

The path leads in between smoothly polished boulders through the Prassanó gorge.

clearly. Walk on further through meadows, right past a farm building and 50m eastwards. Then the path swings down left to the stream. Big plane trees and salmon pink oleander bushes line the banks on both sides. After a short time the stream joins a larger river coming from the south. It's best to cross over now onto the right-hand side. Already steep rock faces flank the river course completely shaded by plane trees. Then the riverbed becomes narrower. Large smoothly polished boulders pile up with water caught in between. If you do the walk in spring you will come across beautiful bathing pools. After 3 hrs. gorge walking the rocks suddenly recede and the landscape opens up. Walk for another hour in the riverbed and then climb up left to a path which leads through olive groves. After ½ hr. you come to some greenhouses and a road which goes under the main highway and meets the old road to Réthimnon at **Missíria**.

Go for a swim in the sea and catch one of the frequent buses back to town.

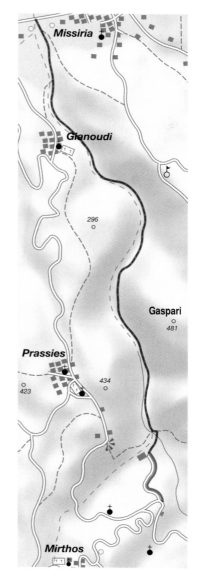

16 Tsiríta gorge

In the valleys to the north of the Kédhros mountains

Patsós – Antonius cave – Tsiríta gorge

Starting point: Patsós, beautifully located village in Réthimnon's hinterland with a large Turkish well, 8km from the road between Amári and Réthimnon.
Walking time: village square to the start of the walk ¾ hr., walk through the gorge ¾ hr., end of the gorge to the road 20 mins. Total time 2 hrs.
Difference in height: ascent 50m, descent 300m.
Grade: easy gorge walk except for a short section at the end. Depending on the level of water you might need to wade through in some places.
Stops and accommodation: two tavernas in Patsós, a taverna at the start of the gorge and two on the road, a large choice of rooms in Réthimnon.
Bus services: once a day from Réthimnon to Patsós and returning after a short stop, Réthimnon – Agia Galíni three a day, two for the return.

The village of Patsós lies in a very fertile hilly region north of the Kédhros massif at a height of 500m. The Tsiríta has carved a short, but for walkers very attractive, narrow gorge through the rock below the village. The top part of the gorge has always been well visited especially because of the Antonius chapel. The walk in the gorge has not yet been completed but if short sections of scrambling over boulders and wading through water do not bother you, it is possible to get through providing, of course, that the water level is low enough.

From the **village square** take the road towards Karínes (west). At the second turn-off a concrete road goes down right. It follows a water channel at first, then goes right at the first fork, left at the next one (10 mins. into the walk) still descending along the water course. After a few minutes you reach a roadway. Descend this for 150m until you come to an old water channel and take the narrow path leading downwards. The start of the gorge can already be seen below. You reach a gravel road at a wide gate on the other side of which there's a sign to the Antonius church. The road ends after 300m by the taverna at the **entrance to the gorge**.

There's a constructed path with wooden railings going down into the narrow gorge and wooden steps lead to an area with a well where you can take a rest. The Antonius chapel is behind this, built close to an overhanging rock face. The deeply cut streambed is at times impassable and the path traverses high above. After about 20 mins. it goes back down to the water again, over to the other side

View into the Tsiríta gorge.

of the stream and past some beautiful waterfalls. Until the path is finished it is only possible to walk the gorge when the water level is low – even then there are some places where you have to wade thigh-deep in the water and climb down over fairly large boulders. The **walk through the gorge** takes about ¾ hr. and then the valley suddenly opens out. The path now runs along by the stream, under plane trees and through oleander bushes, and onto flatter ground. Go on the left side down the stream and up above you can see an agricultural building, then you come to a gravel road. Past an old water mill continue down the valley on the left-hand side. Shortly after the mill there's a road to the right over an old bridge to the village of Voleónes. After just 1km straight on you reach the **tarmac road**. Go along this to the right for another kilometre until you come to some houses with a petrol station and a bus stop, as well as 2 tavernas.

If you've got your own car and would like to see the gorge from above, follow the road from Patsós in the direction of Karínes. A short way from Patsós you come to the first fork in the road on a wide right hand bend going down to the gate mentioned above and to the taverna at the start of the gorge (2.5km).

17 To the summit of Koutsotroúlis, 1083m

Walk in the Kouloúkonas mountains

Kámpos Apladianá – Apladianá – Koutsotroúlis

Starting point: Apladianá, 250m, small village in the valley of the Milopótamos

river north of the Psilorítis massif, 16km from Peramá.

Walking time: Kámpos Apladianá – Apladianá 20 mins., Apladianá – cistern ½ hr., cistern – col 1 hr., col – first summit 1 hr., first summit – main summit ¾ hr. Total time 6 – 6½ hrs.

Difference in height: 800m.

Grade: easy, but strenuous mountain walk, mostly on steep slopes with no paths, very hot in summer, hardly any shade, no water along the way.

Stops and accommodation: rooms in Apladianá and Kámpos Apladianá, tavernas in all the villages along the old road, many shops, tavernas, kafenía and rooms in the small town of Peramá.

Bus services: twice a day on the old road from Réthimnon to Iráklion and return.

Tip: Melidóni cave near Peramá, Minoan villas of Tylissos near Agios Mámas, mountain village of Axos (remains of a large Dorian town).

The river valley of Peramá to the east offers a luxuriant and unique orchard landscape with orange and lemon groves, dense woodland, vineyards and occasional piles of smoking charcoal. The Kouloúkonas mountains form a glaring contrast – barren, dry and deserted – but there's a beautiful view on all sides.

The starting point for the mountain walk is **Kámpos Apladianá** on the old road to Iráklion from which there's another road leading to the somewhat higher **Apladianá**. From the kafénion follow the village road to the church and above to the cemetery. The path goes up to the massif across many terraces and beneath olive trees. Go towards the distinct cleft of a valley. At the end of the olive grove the path follows a wire-netting fence, goes to the right across a streambed and up to a large **cistern** above. Looking back you now have a nice view over the village, the valley and the Psilorítis massif in the

Charcoal burners damping down the fires in the Milopótamos river valley.

south. Follow the newly laid gravel road for a while until you see a goat path on the left hand side going up into the valley cleft. Continue along a dry streambed. The luxuriant flora has now finished and there are vast expanses of vegetation typical for dry areas – small oaks, cistus, herbs of all kinds and sage especially. Follow the narrow path for ¾ hr. steeply up to the top, the last half directly in the rocky streambed, and at a height of 700m you come to a small flat **col** with some large trees and an old sheep pen. Nearby there's a stone shepherd's hut with a dome-shaped roof. Continue up the slope diagonally left to the ridge running east. Through low scrub, over rocks and scree you arrive at the ridge after ¼ hr. and follow this to the **first summit**. Walk for about 40 mins., almost on a level, along the ridge which bends round in a semi-circle, until you reach the summit stone of **Koutsotroúlis**, 1083m. A beautiful panoramic view awaits you with rounded mountain domes and silhouettes, one after the other, until they disappear into the blue coastal mist. The broad and mighty Psilorítis, on the other hand, is a barrier to the views in the south.

For the return you can choose either the same path or, more interestingly although longer, a narrow path which winds down between the first and main summit into the small valley. It crosses the slope below the first summit and meets the other path again on the col at the shepherd's hut.

18 From Vosakóu monastery to Sissés

Marble, monastery and oranges

Kámbos Doxaró – Moni Vosakóu – Sissés

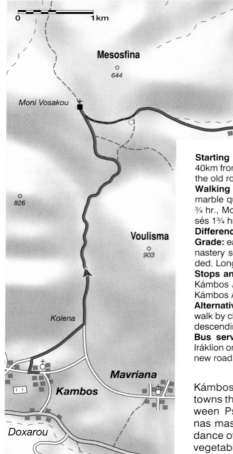

Starting point: Kámbos Doxaró, about 40km from Réthimnon towards Iráklion on the old road.

Walking time: Kámbos Doxaró – col/ marble quarry ¾ hr., col – Moni Vosakóu ¾ hr., Moni Vosakóu – gravel road – Sissés 1¾ hrs. Total time 3¼ hrs.

Difference in height: 150m.

Grade: easy walk. From the Vosakóu monastery some route-finding ability is needed. Long trousers. Plenty of water.

Stops and accommodation: tavernas in Kámbos Apladianá and Sissés, rooms in Kámbos Apladianá and Báli.

Alternative: combine with the previous walk by climbing up the Koutsotroúlis and descending to the Vosakóu monastery.

Bus services: twice daily Réthimnon – Iráklion on the old road, every ½ hr. on the new road.

Kámbos Doxaró is one of many towns that lie in the fertile valley between Psilorítis and the Kouloúkonas massif. The area has an abundance of water and you will see that vegetables and fruit are being culti-

The well-preserved ruins of Vosakóu monastery on the way to Sissés.

vated, together with vines. You might even be lucky enough to come across charcoal burners at work.

Leave **Kámbos Doxaró** to the west where, immediately after a bridge and opposite the church, a gravel road turns off. It climbs slowly southwards and after 45 minutes goes past a marble quarry on the hillside opposite. From the ridge of the pass the road continues for a while, almost at the same height, before gradually dropping down and swinging to the right round a broad hollow (Eso Kámbos) on its way to the **Vosakóu monastery**. (Now look ahead to where the path will go later. As you descend the road you can see opposite a side valley. There's a field path leading through the hollow to this valley with a mountain behind it. Later on you will go round this mountain to the left.) After 1½ hrs. you come to **Moni Vosakóu** situated at the northern end of the Eso Kámbos. Today it's only used by shepherds and you can study at leisure the type of construction with its round archways, steps and stone ornaments.

Leave the monastery at the main gate and go eastwards along an old path. It soon leads to a roadway which ends at a cistern. A field path crosses over beforehand. Go up left on an overgrown path (sheep pens on the left) and cross straight over the small plateau which is surrounded by walls. A gravel road leads down the right-hand side of a valley going eastwards to a farmstead.

Continue left below it and then right at the fork onto the roadway which eventually goes above and parallel to the main road. Keep as long as possible to the right above the main road before going down onto it. Follow the main road for a short while until the start of a crash barrier. A path goes up here into the village of **Sissés** which is famous for its large juicy navel oranges.

South-west Crete

The west and south coasts of Crete are thinly populated, mountainous and even inpenetrable in places. There are many villages tucked away from the stream of tourists and it takes the walker a long time to reach them as well. The area of tourist importance is along the road from Kastélli via Perivólia to **Hrissoskalítissas**, where there's one of the most beautifully situated monasteries in Crete, and to the furthest south-western point, the **Elafónissos islands**.

Paleohóra, the first important town on the south coast, is accessible on a good connecting road from the north via Voukoliés and Kándanos. This lively town has always been popular with hikers. Relatively cheap rooms, beautiful beaches as well as quaint tavernas, cafés and bars provide all you could wish for. Added to that there are boats to Kastélli, the island of Gávdos, Soúgia and Elafónissos.

For many years **Soúgia** was a closely guarded secret amongst those who knew Crete well. The remote village can only be reached via a long mountain road from the north and is built close to the lovely shingle beach before the rocky precipices of the White Mountains make it impossible to get further along the coast, unless you are an experienced hiker. In the meantime the village has grown and visitors are attracted by a good choice of rooms, lots of tavernas, beautiful bays, and a varied, interesting hinterland for excursions and walks. The frescos of Pagoménos here in Moní church are worth a visit but the ancient shrine of Asklepios in **Lissós** can only be reached on foot.

The boat trip along the steep coastline to the east is stunning. It goes close to the coast and gives you fascinating glimpses into the mountain area. The port to aim for is **Agia Rouméli**, the starting point for the walk into the **Samariá gorge**. Indeed there is no other place that has been so radically transformed by tourist development. Agia Rouméli was once a small practically inaccessible village whereas today more than 6000 visitors are dropped off, fed and transferred on.

The hiking path going east brings you to **Loutró** along the most beautiful part of the whole of the south coast. In the bay was the port of ancient Phoenix which used to sit just above the peninsula – a town with more than 20,000 inhabitants. The ancient sites, in **Arádhena** higher up as well, the gorges, mountain villages and a magical landscape provide inviting opportunities for swimming and walking.

You can also take a boat on to **Hóra Sfakíon**. On the journey you'll see many popular beaches. The big town at the south-eastern edge of the White Mountains is a tourist interchange just like Agia Rouméli. Thousands of people transfer daily from the boat to the bus. From here you can return to the north coast over the **Askífou plain** or go eastwards following the coast road

Fishing boats in Agia Galíni harbour.

past the castellations of the Venetian fortress of **Frango Kástello**. The road then leads well above the coast through countless small villages which seem like green oases below the barren mountains.

At the narrowest point of Western Crete the road reaches **Plakiás**, the next large town. Many hotels, tavernas and rooms for rent have spread outside the village around the wide-sweeping bay. It's worth making a visit to the beautiful mountain villages in the surrounding area and some are reached through narrow and high gorges, but **Préveli monastery** with its palm beach is especially worthwhile. The good main road from Réthimnon goes through **Spíli** below the Kédhros mountains and on to **Agia Galíni**. The beautiful countryside is ideal for swimming and walking, and there are tavernas here where you can easily find a room for the night. Agia Galíni, lying on the western edge of the **Messará plain**, is the most established beach resort and port on the south coast of Western Crete.

The countryside now has a completely different character. The previously dominant mountains now fade into the background and are replaced by greenhouses and luxuriant vegetation. On the southern edge of the plain another much-visited beach resort has established itself. Formerly a meeting place for hippies, who often wintered in the caves as well, **Mátala** is today a destination for package tours and consequently overcrowded. The very busy road at this point goes past **Agia Triáda** and **Festós** eastwards through the gently rising Messará plain. On the left, almost hidden by gathering clouds, is the imposing Psilorítis massif. Past **Górtys**, the former Roman provincial capital, the road goes through the hilly main wine growing area of Crete to the flat north coast at Iráklion. On the right hand edge, the **Asteroússia mountains** mark the boundary of the Messará plain and offer the walker a whole series of worthwhile excursions.

19 From Elafónissos to Paleohóra

Along the coast and across Cape Kríos in south-western Crete

Elafónissos – Cape Kríos – Giálos – Paleohóra

Starting point: Elafónissos, car park before the kiosks on the beach with lots of sun umbrellas. E4 signs.

Walking time: Elafónissos – Agios Ioánnis 2¾ hrs., Agios Ioánnis – gravel road 1¼ hrs., gravel road – start of the tarmac road 1 hr., tarmac road – Paleohóra 2 hrs. Total time 7 hrs.

Difference in height: 100m.

Grade: easy walk, but demanding stamina. Sure-footedness needed at times.

Stops and accommodation: in Hrissoskalítissas, Elafónissos and Paleohóra.

Bus services: Kastélli – Moni Hrissoskalítissas (as far as Elafónissos in the tourist season), Paleohóra – Haniá. In the summer / spring daily boats Paleohóra – Elafónissos.

Boat connections: in the summer / spring daily boats Paleohóra – Elafónissos.

The south-west corner of Crete is one of the most enchanting destinations on the island. The Elafonísi islands with their white sand dunes and shallow turquoise water are particularly delightful.

Walk along the beach to the east. About 100 metres after the last bay adorned with sun umbrellas you will see an *E4 sign* on the sea-polished. Continue along by the sea over the flat rock pavements (be sure to find the next E4 sign). The next stage of the walk is confusing. Next to the *E4 signs* there are also *black and yellow waymarkers* on rocks as well as *cairns*. After a good 30 mins. the strenuous stretch of rock comes to an end and the path runs mainly along the sand and through scrub and dunes near to the water. In just

under an hour you reach a cistern, a makeshift hut and some juniper trees. At the end of a long beach the path climbs up over a rocky headland and back down to the sea. After a maze of small boulders it turns at a right angle away from the sea and uphill along a dry streambed (gorge). Up several small rock steps and then a distinct *black and yellow arrow* shows the way. After about 200m the path leaves the valley to the right and goes across the slope about 40m above the sea. On steep ground with lots of ups-and-

Hrissoskalítissas monastery, robbed of its former tranquility.

downs, sometimes over boulders, you finally descend to the sea. After about 2 hrs. you come to a long stretch of beach and the path goes uphill across a slope at the end. After 2¾ hrs. you arrive at the **Agios Ioánnis chapel** (the spring is 50m higher).

20 mins. after the spring continue over steep rocky ground and then go down into a small bay. At the end of the bay, just before some large boulders, go up the slope covered in bushes to a road. The path goes below the road to the flat col of **Cape Kríos** then down the slope over rock steps directly to the shingle beach at **Giálos**.

From here walk along the gravel road as it bends sharply to the left and continue on the tarmac road for about 10km to **Paleohóra**. You can either phone for a taxi or hitch a lift back.

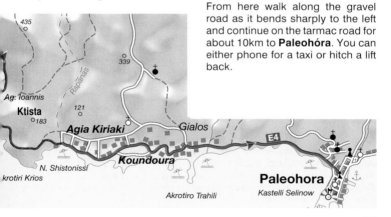

20 From Paleohóra to Soúgia

Along the coast of the Libyan Sea to the Asklepios shrine in Lissós

Paleohóra – Lissós – Soúgia

Starting point: road to the campsite in Pa-
leohóra.
Walking time: Paleohóra – Lissós 3 hrs.,
Lissós – Soúgia 2 hrs.
Total time 5 hrs.
Difference in height: 300m.

Grade: easy walk, but requiring some
stamina. Take sufficient water.
Stops and accommodation: restaurants
and rooms in Paleohóra and Soúgia.
Bus services: Haniá – Paleohóra and
Haniá – Soúgia.

The first part of the path runs directly by the sea so there are plenty of temp-
tations to stop and swim. Then it's goodbye to the beach for a while as the
path goes over a ridge and finishes through a small gorge.
Leave **Paleohóra** to the east on the road to the campsite. After half an hour
walking beside the sea (Anidri beach) the roadway turns into a footpath. After another 2 hours the path ascends, to climb up over a promontory jutting
out into the sea (Cape Flomes). At the top you come to a roadway which, after 10 mins., meets a broad roadway. Go across this and over limestone
and in between junipers, until you come down to the bay of ancient **Lissós**.
This town was once well-known for its Asklepios shrine, which was still re-
vered in Roman times. Although the archaeological site is fenced off, there's
a statue of Pan on display in the archaeological museum in Haniá which
was found here.
On the way to the delightful little bay you will come across a small Byzantine
church with a lot of ancient stone built into its walls.

On the way to Soúgia by the Libyan Sea.

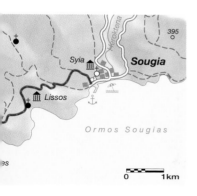

The path to Soúgia continues from this ancient site on the right next to the mosaic floor, at first over a mountain plateau, then downhill into a gorge overgrown with pine trees. Continue along the stream-bed till you reach the harbour of fishing boats and **Soúgia** with its beautiful shingle beach just 5 mins. further on.

21 Agia Iríni gorge to Soúgia

On the western edge of the White Mountains

Agia Iríni – Soúgia

Starting point: Agia Iríni, 650m. The village lies just below the road from Haniá to Soúgia at the start of a deep gorge on the western edge of the White Mountains, about 30km from Soúgia.

Walking time: Agia Iríni – resting place 1 hr., picnic area – end of gorge (café) 1½ hrs., end of gorge – Soúgia 1½ hrs. Total time 4 hrs.

Difference in height: 650m.

Grade: easy gorge walk, very easy route finding, several stream crossings, and so not possible after extended periods of rain, good paths. From the end of the gorge to Soúgia very hot in summer.

Stops and accommodation: choice of rooms, tavernas and cafés in Soúgia.

Bus services: Haniá – Soúgia several times a day. The bus stops for tourists at the entrance of the gorge.

Boat connections: Paleohóra – Soúgia –

Agia Rouméli twice a day.

Tip: ancient site of Lissós, at Rodováni the ancient site of Elíros.

The small village of Agia Iríni lies at a height of 650m in a narrow valley on the windy road from Haniá to Soúgia. If you have come from the Omalós plain and tried in vain to walk the Samariá gorge you will find the **Agia Iríni** gorge just as attractive an alternative for reaching the south coast through extraordinary mountain scenery.

At the south end of the village at a big information board an old traders' path goes steeply down left past a newly constructed resting place with a taverna (with a shop). The path continues on the right-hand side of an almost constantly

Magnificent white anemone blossoms in the Agia Iríni gorge.

running stream towards the start of the gorge (do not cross over the bridge). The path changes sides frequently as it descends through dense woodland and at times on old pathways with steps and supporting walls. After about 45 mins. on the left a little above some ruins, there's a newly built stone house and a signpost to a former partisan hide-out. A narrow path leads from here up to the Omalós plain.

After about an hour you reach a picnic area and from here there's a newly constructed path. The remaining route is well signed with distance markers, red waymarkers, arrows and cairns and there are also several **rest areas** with water and toilets.

The path often goes uphill but almost immediately returns to the valley bottom. The flowers ahead are truly stunning – alpine violets, lilies and anemones. In some places you have to use your hands to scramble over fairly large boulders. After 2½ hrs. of walking the gorge opens out. Olive groves, cultivated terraces and agricultural land indicate the first village. Down the left-hand side of the stream you eventually reach a gravel road with a large car park and taverna (the bus to Soúgia leaves from here in the tourist season).

A small white chapel stands above the road and you can see the archway of a Venetian bridge over the stream below you. (On your return follow the blue arrows here at the junction.) The gravel road leads into a tarmac road next to a bridge and goes left up to the village of Livadás, but you go right and over the bridge to reach **Soúgia** in half an hour.

22 From Soúgia to Agia Rouméli

A demanding alpine walk at the foot of the White Mountains and an easier variation

Soúgia – Agios António turn-off – Tripití fortress – Tripití gorge – Sentóni beach – Donáta beach – Cape Kalotrivídis – Agia Rouméli

Starting point: Soúgia on the south coast at the end of the road between Haniá and Soúgia. An elongated beautiful shingle beach broadens out in front of many tavernas and cafés.

Walking times: Soúgia – Agios António turn-off 2½ hrs., turn-off – Tripití fortress 2 hrs., Tripití fortress – Tripití gorge ¾ hr., Tripití gorge – Sentóni beach ½ hr., Sentóni beach – Donáta beach 3 hrs., Donáta beach – Cape Kalotrivídis 3 hrs., Cape Kalotrivídis – Agia Rouméli 2½ hrs. Total time 14 hrs. (2 days).

Difference in height: ascents and descents 1000m each, including a long incline of 560m.

Grade: this stage of the European long distance path (E4) is one of the most demanding walks on the whole of Crete. The walker needs a good sense of direction.

Some steep ascents and descents lie ahead, together with repeated exposed sections where sure-footedness and a lack of vertigo are absolutely essential. There are also long sections without shade with merciless sun and heat and hardly any drinking water on the way.

You should definitely plan to spend a night on the beach for which you will need to carry additional water. There are sufficient E4 signposts, yellow-black and red way-markings.

Stops and accommodation: tavernas, cafes and rooms for rent in Soúgia and Agia Rouméli.

Bus connections: daily between Haniá and Soúgia

Boat connections: in the season Paleohóra – Soúgia – Agia Rouméli daily; several a day Agia Rouméli – Hora Sfakíon.

Alternative: if you find this walk too long

and strenuous, you can easily enjoy just a part of it. The section from Soúgia to the turn-off to the chapel of Agios António and down to the little church is an easy walk, in contrast to the longer route, with magnificent scenery and it can be recommended as a day walk with a stop for a swim. But it can also be very hot here from spring onwards; sturdy walking shoes and enough drinking water are therefore also very necessary.

The largest part of the path is identical to the main one described next. For the detour to the Agios António chapel go past the chapel above it along the E4. When you can't see the little church any more, follow an indistinct path marked with cairns branching off right. Underneath some largish trees first go downhill, directly towards the coast. At a steeper slope

you will find a piece of the old paved path; it leads you close to some rocks for a little way to the west. The narrow path leads you for the last 5 minutes again underneath some large trees to the south and out onto the flat peninsula. Big olive trees, a clearing and the two-naved little church of **Agios António** lie ahead (20 mins. from the E4).

A lovely place to stop and rest – the view of the sea, flat slabs of rock, shingle islands and many small pools and narrow water channels are continually washed over by the surf. When the waves are high you must be careful when swimming, as there are rocks everywhere; water sandals are an advantage.

For the return, go directly along beside the water across the flat slabs of rock in a westerly direction. Still in sight of the chapel, at the first large boulder right by the water, make another stop and you will find in the shingle several small springs with clear water, the strongest at the front below the rock. Stay close to the water and after about 15 minutes you come to the end of

the flat peninsula.

Reddish brown breaks in the rock seem to bar further progress. Near to the water where remains of walls are tucked in close to the rock, go directly past the rock on the left and find an old path which leads you in 5 minutes through the break in the rock up to the top to an old threshing circle. On a narrow rocky ledge about 30m above the sea go to the left, at first gently uphill, then on the level, continuing almost at the same height to the west around the next sheer drop where numerous cairns show you the way.

The terrain broadens out into the valley floor, the vegetation increases and before the first little wood a track leads away from the sea up the flat valley. Below large trees, left past another threshing circle, you come to the path you will recognise from the start at a large pile of stones (E4).

Straight ahead brings you into the gorge and after 15 minutes going uphill along the old bridle path you reach the col again.

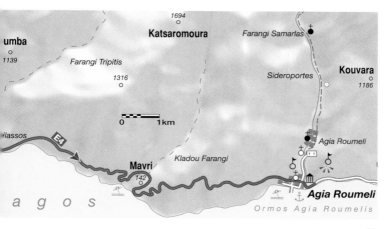

At the eastern edge of **Soúgia** village, after the last houses on the beach, an *E4 waymarker* post indicates the route directly along the broad dry stony bed of the river. This is where the demanding and scenically beautiful coastal walk begins. Go diagonally across the streambed uphill. After about 100m you can see a red waymarker on a wall. Along fences, uphill over flat terraces with gnarled olive trees, you meet a gravel road after a short steeper section. Leave the road again on a left-hand bend on a small path (*E4 sign*) to the right and come onto it again a little above. Follow it along until it ends at a height of about 130m on a flat small plateau with a beautiful view of the bay of Soúgia. A path goes from here gently downhill through bushes towards the sea and eventually at a height of about 90m goes eastwards amongst evergreens parallel to the coast. The path turns to the left above the second bay into a small valley. After a rather steep incline in a small gorge it reaches a col covered with pines (160m). Shortly before this a turn-off leads up into the mountain village of Koustogérako.

Now go round hairpin bends along an old path into the gorge beyond covered in pines, past a cave (with an improvised church inside) and 40m further on go eastwards again after a left-hand bend (just on the right here next to the path, a pyramid of stones marks the return path from the Agios

Soúgia.

António chapel). Continue along the coast over long-abandoned terraces and gradually ascend to the top. About 60m further down, below a steep drop, there's the little **Agios António** chapel on a peninsula. After you have passed the chapel and you can no longer see it, you come to the start of a section where the slope begins to flatten out. It runs down to the coast densely covered in undergrowth and tallish trees. There's a **turn-off** here down to the chapel (see Alternative). The E4 gets closer and closer to the steep ridge of Cape Tripití looming up ahead and leads down to the sea almost as far as a narrow bay. Eventually it goes steeply uphill without paths, across boulders under tall pines to the top until the path finally turns off in the direction of the sea, forces its way through a rock gate at a crossroads and leads to a small, contained spring (only a dribble in summer).

The E4 coastal path.

After a hairpin bend go up across a wide gorse slope onto the col with the ruins of the small Venetian fort of **Tripití**. The ruined remains of the ancient town of Pikilassos lie strewn across the wide hillside.

Continuing uphill directly past the fort you come to the summit chapel of Profítis Ilías with a magnificent viewpoint (there and back 30 mins.).

The path goes from the col steeply downhill over scree in between pines into the Tripití gorge and along a gravel track to the right past two huts to the sea (concrete moorings for boats). Well-marked with *E4 signs* the path leads alongside the sea through a confusion of boulders, over slabs and often through the spray of the surf too (not possible if there's a stormy sea). After this rocky section you come to a small bay with the **Sentóni beach**. After a house with a fence around it, just before the beach, the well-marked path ascends up the hillside by the coast, first across quite a large plain and then again down to the next bay to a height of about 30m.

Go round the bay at this height over broken terrain. The path ascends after that and leads through loose gravel until your way is barred by a gate at a rocky cleft. After climbing up the steep scree slope continue along an airy

Agios Antónios chapel.

band of rock where you need to be sure-footed and have a good head for heights. Afterwards go across a sloping plain, down to a small gorge and uphill again on the other side. Be careful to follow the left-hand turn-off at the fork in the path (the waymarkings are further on), then cross a slope covered with gorse and thyme up to a col (160m) beyond Mávri hill. Continue a bit further across the plain, then steeply downhill into a gorge with gravel walls as far as the sea. Walk along the fine sand and shingle beach of the almost 1km long and beautiful **Donáta bay**.

At the eastern end, well-marked with *E4 signs*, the path goes left up through a small gorge with a steep gradient to the height of the gravel plateau. The path turns off diagonally right there and finally leads up the steep slope covered in low bushes to the 530m high rounded hilltop of Cape Kalotri-vídis. The E4 posts finish here. A narrow path leads into a pinewood, at first on the level crossing the slope, then gradually downhill into a gorge, rarely marked with cairns. Be careful here: 5 minutes after the hilltop the path seems to make a 150 degree bend to the right, is marked with cairns and leads back down again. Do not follow this path; be sure to continue straight on without paths. *Cairns* appear again after about 50m, just as *red waymarkings* and a narrow path which leads under the shade of pines and cypress trees to a valley bottom lying at a height of about 500m. The path goes on the other side of the valley uphill again in the direction of the sea. Go straight on for a short way and then round many hairpin bends further uphill to a rock overhang (570m). From here on the path descends, going gently up and down across a steep hillside towards the sea far below. **Agia Rouméli** appears for the first time and there are *E4 waymarkers* again. Go across fields of scree underneath large pine trees and then steeply downhill, although the path still keeps high above the sea. Now comes an ascent of 50m and afterwards you continue downhill on an exposed path over slippery undergrowth and you cross over to the pinewood directly above Agia Rouméli. Descend steeply, still on a somewhat slippery path, right down to the houses by the sea.

The little church of Agios Pávlos with Agia Rouméli beach in the background.

23 From Agia Rouméli to Hóra Sfakíon

The E4 coastal path

Agia Rouméli – Agios Pávlos – Mármara bay – Loutró – Agios Stavrós – Hóra Sfakíon

Starting point: Agia Rouméli, at the end of the Samariá gorge on a narrow shingle beach situated below the huge steep cliffs of the White Mountains.

Walking time: Agia Rouméli – Agios Pávlos 1¼ hrs., Agios Pávlos – fork in the path 30 mins., fork – Mármara bay 2¼ hrs., Mármara bay – Loutró 1¼ hrs, Loutró – Agios Stavrós 45 mins., Agios Stavrós – start of the roadway 45 mins., roadway – Hóra Sfakíon 45 mins. Total time 7½ hrs.

Difference in height: 600m.

Grade: an easy coastal walk, with a few rocky sections where sure-footedness and a good head for heights are necessary, lengthy stretches on sand and pebbles, sturdy footwear essential, not much shade.

Stops and accommodation: in Agia Rouméli, Fínix, Loutró and Hóra Sfakíon.

Bus services: Hóra Sfakíon – Haniá several times a day, Hóra Sfakíon – Plakiás once a day.

Tip: Sotíros Christós chapel at Loutró on the site of the ancient town of Phoenix on the peninsula – lots of foundation walls, archways and ruins of buildings indicate the extent of this once large town (20,000 inhabitants).

This best known and most beautiful section of the south coast is well-suited for walking due to good accessibility by boat and the many opportunities for stopping at tavernas and for staying overnight. Moreover, the route finding is straightforward and the terrain fairly easy-going. The only drawback is the extreme heat in summer and there are very few places in the shade, so it is advisable in summer and autumn to take sufficient drinking water.

From **Agia Rouméli** start off in the direction of the Samariá gorge. After the last houses the stony path runs parallel to the broad streambed. Cross this at the old bridge and then follow the *cairns* and *E4 waymarkers*. The sandy path goes mainly 20 to 50m above the shingle beach along the dunes to the east. Sometimes stony, sometimes sandy and often over big boulders you

A boat leaving Loutró harbour. Hóra Sfakíon in the distance.

walk quite a way under large pine trees across the slope. Finally you drop down to the beach of sand and pebbles and reach the little church of **Agios Pávlos** after 1¼ hrs. (a small taverna just in front). Directly below the church

At the exit from the Arádhena gorge.

cold spring water pours out of the sand right into summer. When the sea is rough these places are flooded. Here's the last chance for a swim as the path now goes over the top of the cliff.

Just behind the church go steeply up the sand dune for a short while to the path which continues under large pine trees. With a wide view down onto the sea 100m below you walk on mostly level ground until you come to the turn-off to **Agios Ioánnis**, about 30 mins. from the church. Stay on the lower path which leads in a few minutes to a large cistern. Contour into a gorge coming from above on a rather exposed rocky path which reaches the highest point of 150m and then continues across the open slope. 2 hrs. after the fork in the road you come to the bottom of the deep rugged Arádhena gorge which opens out into a wonderful little rocky bay, the **Mármara bay**. White marble benches and turquoise water attract sun seekers from the neighbouring Loutró. Past newly built stone houses (drinks, snacks) a short steep descent leads directly into the bay. Take a quick look left between the two steep walls of the Arádhena gorge before continuing up over slabs of rock.

The last steep section is the hardest of the whole walk. The exposed path goes very close to the 50m cliff along a terraced piece of ground and drops down steeply to the sea. You will need to use your hands to scramble down this descent. Now continue towards the already visible houses along the beach, directly across the terrace of the last taverna and up the steps to the slope above. You have to go over another hill and then you can see the village of Livaniáná above on the steep slope and below the idyllic taverna of Fínix where the ancient port of the town of the same name once stood. There's a short climb up to the remarkable ruins of the Venetian fort from where you have a wonderful view down onto the picturesque village of **Loutró** below. After descending for 10 mins. you can be sitting in one of the tavernas at the port.

At the eastern edge, by the Tokrikri taverna, the path goes up the slope to the left behind the village (*red waymarkers*) and continues at a similar height to the east with fantastic views. After the descent to a fairly long stretch of beach the path goes above the sea close to the chapel of **Agios Stavrós** (45 mins. from Loutró). A short steep descent brings you to a bay again with several freshwater springs (in summer there's a kiosk and boat service to Hóra Sfakíon and Loutró).

Make your way rather laboriously over rocks and pebbles to a steep cliff and beyond on a path cut into the rocks. A few zigzags lead you up onto the road from Anópolis. The rather monotonous tarmac road brings you in 45 mins. to **Hóra Sfakíon**.

Inlingías bay is the last place for a marvellous swim before Hóra Sfakíon.

24 From Agia Rouméli to Hóra Sfakíon

Above the Libyan Sea and under the White Mountains

Agia Rouméli – Agios Ioánnis – Arádhena – Anópolis – Hóra Sfakíon

Starting point: Agia Rouméli at the end of the Samariá gorge.

Walking time: Agia Rouméli – junction Agios Ioánnis / Loutró 1½ hrs., junction – Agios Ioánnis 2½ hrs., Agios Ioánnis – Arádhena 1 hr., Arádhena – Anópolis 1 hr., Anópolis – Hóra Sfakíon 2 hrs.
Total time 8 hrs.

Difference in height: 800m.

Grade: stamina required. Long climb to Agios Ioánnis. Take sufficient water with you.

Stops and accommodation: restau-rants / rooms in Agia Rouméli, Anópolis and Hóra Sfakíon (Walk 23). Kafeníon in Agios Ioánnis.

Alternative: instead of going up to Agios Ioánnis, walk by the sea to Hóra Sfakíon. From Arádhena it's possible to descend the gorge to the sea and continue along the coast.
Instead of descending from Anópolis to Hóra Sfakíon, descend to Loutró and continue along the coast to Hóra Sfakíon.

Bus services: several buses a day fom Hóra Sfakíon to Haniá.

The start of the walk to the **turn-off to Agios Ioánnis** is identical to Walk 23. Turn left here from the coastal path (*signed yellow*)! The path winds its way steeply upwards and broadens out after more than an hour of exhausting climbing until the old paving stones come into view. Still gently ascending the path goes through pine and cypress trees to the church of Panagia, (right) just before **Agios Ioánnis**. There are some pretty ceiling frescos in the little chapel on the left. Just where the path meets the new road to Arádhena they have made a kafení-on out of an old school. Choose either to take the road (5km to Arádhena) or the partly paved path which runs below the road. The village at the top of the Arádhena gorge is almost abandoned but the church of the Archangel Michael is worth a visit. You come to the other side of the gorge across the new steel bridge. 800m after the bridge the path turns off the roadway to the right to **Anópolis**. There are two ka-fenía in the village and as you leave in the direction of Anópolis, a res-taurant too. Leave Anópolis on the tarmac road to Hóra Sfakíon. Conti-nue for 10 minutes after the sign for

The new steel girder bridge over the Arádhena gorge.

the end of the village till you see on a hairpin bend a gravel road going down left to a little pump house (long shed opposite). Take the first turn-off right. The roadway ends at the second pump station and continues as a path (cairns) into a gorge. Stay first on the right, then on the left and later walk in the valley bottom. An hour after you have left Anópolis you come to a wide gorge leading down to the sea (**Inlingías gorge**). Opposite you will see the path that takes you to **Hóra Sfakíon** in half an hour.

25 Through the Arádhena gorge into the mountain village of Anópolis

Round walk from Loutró via Arádhena to Anópolis

Loutró – Mármara bay – Arádhena – Anópolis – Loutró

Starting point: Loutró, idyllic village on the south coast between Hóra Sfakíon and Agia Rouméli, can only be reached by boat or on foot.

Walking time: Loutró – Mármara bay 1¼ hrs., Mármara bay – gorge walk to Arádhena 2¼ hrs., Arádhena – Anópolis 1 hr., Anópolis – Loutró 1¾ hrs. Total time 6-6½ hrs.

Difference in height: 800m.

Grade: long walk without good paths but easy route finding.

Difficult gorge walk, many short scrambling sections, a fairly high section with two sturdy iron ladders. Good footwear necessary, some shade in the gorge but mostly sunny. Drinking water available in the tavernas and villages as well as from the spring in the gorge. Possible all year round.

Stops and accommodation: many tavernas and b&b in Loutró, Fínix and Anópolis. Hotel Plátanos.

Bus services: several a day to Hóra Sfakíon, twice a day to Anópolis.

Boat connections: several a day to Loutró.

Tip: ruins of the ancient town of Arádhena and the Agia Kateríni chapel above Anópolis with a wonderful view.

At the western edge of **Loutró** a footpath leads from the harbour and zig-zags up the steep slope, crosses the hill, goes past the large cistern and the Fínix bay above the Sífis taverna. Cross another hill (turn-off to the village of Livplaniá, marked blue) and descend to the taverna (red waymarkers), go over the terrace and a short way along the beach. A short climb follows and after a 10 minute traverse you soon descend into **Mármara bay** for a refreshing swim (E4 markings up to this point).

Walk away from the shingle beach along the streambed into the **Arádhena gorge**. Partly overhanging yellowy and reddish rock faces tower up 200m on either side. The first part of the gorge is very shady and pleasant even in summer. The path goes gently up the narrow gorge over gravely stones. Boulders and dense undergrowth hinder your progress and you frequently need to use your hands. There are cairns to guide you along unclear paths. After 45 mins. walking you will discover a small spring under a large boulder. Another 15 mins. past this you come to a fairly large **basin-shaped valley** (you can climb up the right-hand side to the village of Livianá).

The valley narrows again and the gorge winds up into the mountains. The necessity to climb over large, solid limestone boulders becomes more frequent. Suddenly, in the upper part of the gorge after a total of 1¾ hrs., the path is blocked by huge boulders. You used to have to climb up the 12m high barrier with the help of old ropes and a massive iron chain. Today it's less of a struggle to the top. After that it's a strenuous climb for 20 mins. over relatively steep boulders and scree until you can see the new iron bridge for the Anópolis – Arádhena road high above. Only another 15 mins. to the old footpath which traverses the gorge. On the left-hand side of the gorge the lovely paved path winds up into **Arádhena**, situated at 600m and built on the ruins of the ancient town. The church of Archangel Michael is worth visiting with its well-preserved frescos dating back to 1546.

Go through the ruins onto the roadway and cross the iron bridge (there's a drinks' van at the western end of the bridge in summer) to the other side of the gorge in the direction of **Anópolis**. Either continue on this gravel road (3.5km) to the beautifully situated mountain village or after 500m follow the *red waymarkings* on your right along an old paved footpath which will take you to Anópolis in the same time. Anópolis occupies the whole of the green valley and up till now has kept its quiet remote character despite the first signs of tourism.

From the village square – in the centre the memorial to the resistance fighter Daskalojannis – walk past the taverna and follow the narrow tarmac road to-

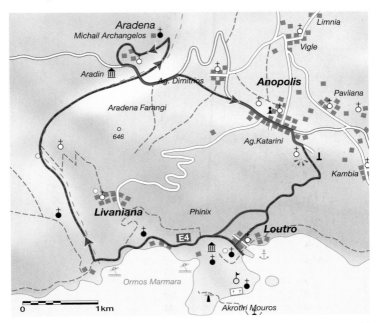

wards the southern edge of the village. An old footpath at the last house goes south-east up the steep hill. At the top (10 mins.) the path divides. It's worth making a detour 100m higher to the little church of **Agia Kateríni** from which there's a wonderful view of the south coast and the whole length of the walk. Follow the winding path straight down to Loutró 650m below. 10 mins. from the eastern edge of Anópolis, a path joins from the left below the chapel.

The breathtaking rock faces of the Arádhena gorge.

Anópolis lies in the bottom of a spacious, very fertile valley.

Just before Loutró there's a turn-off (the red waymarkers lead to the penin-sula above Loutró where the ruined fortress is situated) and you go left down to **Loutró** (15 mins.).

26 Livanianá and the Arádhena gorge

Round walk from Fínix via Livanianá into the gorge

Fínix – Livanianá – Arádhena gorge – Mármara bay – Fínix

Starting point: Fínix, once the port for ancient Phoenix, west of Loutró (the next bay after the ridge). A chapel and two tavernas where you can stay overnight, directly by the sea, 30 mins. from Loutró.

Walking time: Fínix – Livanianá 1 hr., Livanianá – Arádhena gorge ¾ hr., Arádhena gorge – Mármara bay 1 hr., Mármara bay – Fínix ¾ hr. Total time 3½ hrs.

Difference in height: 350m.

Grade: walk of moderate difficulty, sometimes without paths, some easy climbing in the gorge over large rocks, short exposed sections along the coast. Only a little shade, possible all year round (in summer you are advised to make a break earlier because of the heat).

Stops and accommodation: rooms and lots of tavernas in Loutró.

Bus services: Vrísses – Hóra Sfakíon several times a day. In the tourist season a boat from Hóra Sfakíon via Loutró to Agia Rouméli several times a day. Sifis ferries his guests on request by boat to and from Loutró or Hóra Sfakíon.

Tip: the hill between Loutró and Fínix was the site for the big town of Phoenix (20,000 inhabitants), many foundation walls and ruins of buildings with the beautifully situated Sotíros Christós chapel.

The path climbs gently upwards directly from Sífis' **taverna** at the water's edge and in a few minutes meets the path between Loutró and Agia Rouméli at the top of a small hill. While the route coming down from Loutró leads to the next taverna your path continues with blue markings up the increasingly steep slope. A little higher up the new road goes to the village. The old path was once well-used – it is wide, paved and has supporting walls. The path arrives in **Livanianá** above the houses on the right and leads into the village. Zigzags and steps lead up to the church, the highest point of the village at 270m. Next to the church there's a large cistern. Above the church, on the large **slabs of rock**, the path divides. In 20 mins. you can climb up right onto the new road already mentioned and reach Anópolis in another hour. First go left over the flat ridge and then down onto the terraced hillside towards the Arádhena gorge below. After the first gate go immediately left steeply downhill. At the left edge of the steep slope the path goes underneath the reddish rocks towards the valley bottom. Just before reaching the

View down to the fishing village of Loutró situated in an idyllic bay.

bottom it crosses the slope to the right and reaches the dry **streambed** (¾ hr. from the church) at a large solitary olive tree. Now walk down the gorge along the valley bottom. *Cairns* mark the path. After 10 mins. you reach a small spring under large rocks which only provides water sparingly in summer. There's some climbing over large blocks of stone otherwise it's an easy descent along the stony streambed to the sea. You come to **Mármara bay** after 1 hr., a chapel, several small stone houses (food and accomodation). The shingle beach is surrounded with smooth white marble rocks. It is heavily frequented in the tourist season, from midday onwards at the latest, by sunbathers from the neighbouring Loutró who come mostly by boat. In ¾ hr. you return to **Fínix** along the path already described in Walk 23 (*E4 waymarkings*).

27 From Hóra Sfakíon to Anópolis

Through the Inlingías gorge into the mountain village

Hóra Sfakíon – Inlingías gorge – Anópolis

Starting point: Hóra Sfakíon, 60m behind the last house on the road to Anópolis.
Walking time: 2 hrs.
Difference in height: 590m.
Grade: easy walk along an old link path.

Good footwear.
Stops and accommodation: restaurants and rooms in Hóra Sfakíon and Anópolis.
Bus services: Hóra Sfakíon – Anópolis twice a day.

Above the mountain village of Anópolis on the southern slopes of the White Mountains you can still sense the spirit of freedom and independence which the brave people of Sfakíon maintained in their resistance to Turkish rule. From here they drive their cattle onto the barren pastures of the White Mountains and no one knows the paths over the mountains better than they do.

The old path begins 60m behind the last house in **Hóra Sfakíon** on the tarmac road to Anópolis. Go right, up a cliff, to a hidden path which becomes paved a little later on and follow this upwards to a gravel path. Go left to the next fork, then left again, gently uphill to a sharp left hand bend. Here on the right-hand side is the entrance to the **Inlingías gorge**. On the other side go uphill gradually into a side gorge – the **Anópolis gorge**. Ascend this gorge

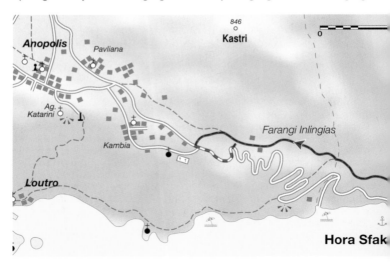

A well-maintained section of the path in the Inlingías gorge.

(first in the bottom, later on the right and then on the left) to the end where you arrive at a **pump station**. From here go along a gravel track past another pump station to a sheep pen. At the third pump station from the gravel track go straight up the path to the tarmac road. Cross this and take the path uphill to the transmitter. Go past this on the right, then along beside a stone wall to a gate. The path comes out at the Tria Adelfia restaurant.

Alternative: at the 3rd pump station on a left-hand bend you come to the tarmac road and along this reach the village. This is well worthwhile since the view of **Hóra Sfakíon** and the south coast as far away as Frango Kástello is spectacular. It's then another 20 mins. from the first houses to the centre of the village.

28 Imbros gorge

A gorge to touch

Komitádes – Imbros gorge – Imbros (Askífou plain)

Starting point: eastern exit from Komitádes, 5km from Hóra Sfakíon.
Walking time: Komitádes – rock arch ½ hr., rock arch – cistern ½ hr., cistern – Imbros 1½ hrs. Total time 2½ hrs.
Difference in height: 580m.
Grade: easy walk along the valley bottom.
Stops and accommodation: restaurant

and rooms in Komitádes, kafeníon and rooms in Imbros.
Alternative: the Askífou plain serves as the starting point for climbing the Kástro.
Bus services: Hóra Sfakíon – Imbros several times a day, Hóra Sfakíon – Komitádes twice a day.
Tip: there's an entrance fee for the gorge walk.

On hardly any other Mediterranean island are there as many gorges as there are on Crete and so you do not have to focus your attention exclusively on the overcrowded Samariá gorge. The walk through the Imbros

At the narrowest part of the Imbros gorge.

gorge near to Hóra Sfakíon is as easy as it is short.

The route begins at the place-name sign at the eastern edge of **Komitádes** (signpost *'to Imbros gorge'*). At first the path goes over river gravel which is not always pleasant. But in 20 mins. the gorge walls converge and 10 mins. later the old paved road which was the traditional connecting route from the north to the south coast emerges and this makes for considerably easier walking. Then your gaze is caught by a huge **rock gateway**. Solitary mountain goats find their way between an increasing number of cypress trees high up on the bare rock faces. You should keep an eye on them since they sometimes dislodge stones.

After a good hour of pleasant climbing you come to a cistern and cattle troughs. The gorge is now so narrow that you can touch the walls with outstretched hands. But soon the rocks recede and the gorge ascends gradually to the top. After walking for 2½ hrs. you reach the houses of **Imbros**. It is the southernmost village on the 780m high plain which is crossed by the pass from Hóra Sfakíon to Vrísses. Walnut trees grow here and potatoes and corn are cultivated as well as vines.

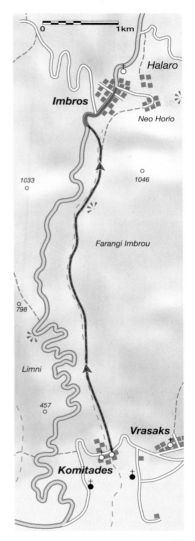

29 Asfendóu gorge

Along century old connecting routes to the south coast

Karés (Askífou plain) – Mesa Goní – Asfendóu – Agios Nektários

Starting point: south-eastern end of the village of Karés (Askífou plain).
Walking time: Karés – Mesa Goní ½ hr., Mesa Goní – col 1¾ hrs., col – Asfendóu 1¼ hrs., Asfendóu – Agios Nektários 1½ hrs. Total time 5 hrs.
Difference in height: ascent 400m, descent 940m.
Grade: easy walk, but demanding stamina. Good footwear, enough provisions.
Stops and accommodation: rooms and tavernas in Amoudári (Askífou plain), Hóra Sfakíon and Frango Kástello.
Alternative: from Asfendóu you can go via Kallikrátis and descend the Kallikratanó gorge to Patsianós (see Walk 30).
Bus services: Vrísses – Karés – Hóra Sfakíon several times a day, Agios Nektários – Hóra Sfakíon once a day.
Tip: 6km from Vrísses it's worth making a detour to the village of Alíkambos, 1km from the pass, where, in the little church of Panagia, you will find unusually well-preserved frescos by the famous Byzan-

tine church painter Pogomenos dating back to 1315-1316.

One of the most impressive stretches of road on Crete is the drive from Haniá to Hóra Sfakíon on the south coast. After the shady village of Vrísses, the meaning of which is something similar to watertaps, located under tall plane trees, the road winds up on seemingly endless zigzags until the pass at 800m gives you an open view over the plain surrounded by mountains. At the northern edge of the Askífou plain is situated the village of Karés (ruins of a Turkish fortress). Just like the other villages of this plain Karés was built right at the edge because of the meltwater and rainwater in winter. One of the oldest connecting routes between the villages of the plain and Asfendóu above the south coast starts here and takes you straight across the fertile plain.

Go away from the tarmac road through the village down to the last house (three flat concrete roofs) at the south-eastern edge. Just behind is where the **old road** begins which has some of the original paving and is still driven along. Start your walk along here across the fertile plain towards Mesa Goní. After a good 500m go first to the left, then to the right into the cleft of the valley below the Turkish fortress. In 25 mins. you reach the village of **Mesa Goní**. Just beforehand, you turn left onto the tarmac road coming from Amoudári. Below, to the left, is situated a cemetery surrounded by cypress trees. The road ascends and leads to the right past the village and through fields into the valley running south. The valley narrows and the gravel road slowly ascends until it finally reaches a sheep pen. Enjoy the wonderful panoramic view. You've been walking for a good 1¼ hrs. There's a fork in the old footpath, nowadays used more by shepherds and their herds, and an arrow points to the left. After 10 mins. a path goes up left (red arrow). Then in another 10 mins. (red markings) you reach a small plateau. The previously lush vegetation has disappeared – rock roses, sage, thyme and oak trees predominate. Go past a cistern with a sheep trough and then between two stately holm oaks ascend a still well-preserved old path zigzagging up to the mountain col ahead. Looking down into the valley below you see an almost intact old path which adapts discreetly to the lie of the land. Past a small plateau with cisterns and sheep pens a gravel road leads down over several plateaus in the direction of **Asfendóu**. Ahead lie the grey houses of Asfendóu. The solitary houses under the big pear trees, the sound of sheep bells and the calling of the shepherds give an impression more of an alpine pasture than a Cretan village.

The gravel road joins the road to Kallikrátis. Follow this for 200m then continue right along a field track leading to the start of the Asfendóu gorge. If instead of the **Asfendóu gorge** you would rather descend the Kallikratianó gorge to the south coast in the direction of Frango Kástello, take the gravel road to Kallikrátis and find the path into the gorge from there (see the following walk). The old descent route through the Asfendóu gorge is distinct and therefore needs no further description. After 1½ hrs. down the right-hand side of the gorge you reach the village of **Agios Nektários**.

30 From Asfendóu through the Kallikratianó gorge to Frango Kástello

Hideouts of the Resistance and escape routes during the Turkish occupation

Asfendóu – Kallikrátis – Kallikratianó gorge – Patsianós – Frango Kástello

Starting point: Asfendóu, see Walk 29.
Walking time: Asfendóu – Kallikrátis 1½ hrs., Kallikrátis – start of the gorge ½ hr., Kallikratianó gorge 1½ hr., Patsianós – Frango Kástello 1 hr. Total time 4½ hrs.
Difference in height: descend 800m.
Grade: easy, but very long walk requiring stamina. Good footwear and sun protection.
Stops and accommodation: two kafenía in Kallikrátis. Restaurants and rooms in Frango Kástello.
Alternative: through the Asfendóu gorge (see Walk 29). A lovely approach to Kallikrátis is possible from Asi Goniá, where a sandy road turns off right from the road to Kallikrátis at the end of the village. It soon turns into a path leading upwards in a gorge where you must twice keep to the right before meeting a road at the top leading to Kallikrátis (2½-3 hrs).
Bus services: Plakiás – Frango Kástello – Hóra Sfakíon once a day.

The starting point for your walk is **Asfendóu** which you come to by following the previous walk. It's best to take the gravel road to Kallikrátis going east. In half an hour it brings you right into the centre of **Kallikrátis** (6km). You should have a look at the church with the sundial and the beautiful well.

Two kafenía are open during the summer, but in winter the village is practically deserted when the inhabitants move down into Kapsodásos or Patsianós at the end of the gorge. The well-improved path down to the coast is still regularly used by the locals, but by car, a wider diversion is necessary to reach both these villages.

Refreshing spring water from the well in Kallikrátis.

Continue your walk to the south at the point where the edge of the valley overlooks the deepest part of the gorge. Looking in this direction you will see on the left a church on top of a hill. To the right of it there's a **dry stream-bed**.

On the left side of this there's a path leading gradually to the start of the gorge. Here you meet a new road which you follow to the left for about ¼ hr. from the stream. Then take the path leading off right (signpost Patsianós/ Frango Kástello) into the streambed. The good old path crosses over the streambed several times – the walking on it is enjoyable. The gorge becomes narrower and the path, concreted in places, steeper. Then the gorge widens into a basin-shaped valley. Steep rock faces enclose you again before the gorge finally opens out after more than an hour from Kallikrátis with a view over the broad coastal plain in front of Frango Kástello. Going past oleander bushes on the right-hand side of the gorge you reach the village of **Patsianós**. Opposite on the left is the village of **Kapsodásos**. To **Frango Kástello** it's another 3km.

In 1828 the fortress, built in the 14th century by the Venetians, was the venue for a bloody battle. 700 Cretan soldiers under the leadership of Chadzimichális were beaten in battle by an army of 8,000 Turks. Every year around 17th May there's a strange ghostly appearance. Just before sunset a long procession of blackly clad riders and figures moves towards Frango Kástello. They say that the phenomena lasts 10 mins. and occurs if, after a few wet days, there's a sudden calm before the north wind begins. The appearance is explained scientifically as a kind of mirage.

31 Villages on the edge of the Kotsifoú gorge

Beautiful view over the Gulf of Plakiás

Plakiás – Sellía; Plakiás – Mírthios

Starting point: in Plakiás, 41km south-west of Réthimnon, at the bridge over the river.
Walking time: Plakiás – Sellía 1 hr.; Plakiás – Mírthios ½ hr.
Difference in height: Sellía 280m, Mírthios 200m.
Grade: easy walks.
Stops and accommodation: tavernas and rooms in Plakiás, Sellía and Mírthios.
Alternative: if you walk from Sellía along the tarmac road to Mírthios (1 hr.) you come to the entrance to the Kotsifoú gorge where you can make a short detour.
Bus services: Plakiás – Réthimnon several daily, Agia Galíni – Plakiás – Hóra Sfakíon once a day.

The town of Plakiás on the south coast of the district of Réthimnon is really worth a visit due to its sur-roundings, the nearby monasteries, its sandy beach and the numerous tavernas. Two short walks into the mountain villages situated above with wonderful views can easily be incorporated into the day's itin-erary.

You begin the short walk to Sellía in **Plakiás** at the bridge over the stream (at the place where the bus turns round). Going into the village turn off right into the street at Zórba's Rent Rooms, go past a few small supermarkets until the road winds into the olive groves. Go left at the first fork. After ¼ hr. go left again at a fork at a bridge and right immediately afterwards. At the next fork (5 mins.) go left, still through olive groves. At the next crossroads go left again and at the following one turn right onto a concrete section. In just un-der an hour you arrive in **Sellía**.

You now have a delightful view over the bay of Plakiás and the surrounding mountains with the village of Mírthios opposite. It's pleasant to sit here a while on the terrace of the Obelistírion taverna.

The walk to Mírthios starts in **Plakiás** too. At the bus turning place go across the little bridge and at Zórba's Rent Rooms take the road which goes at a right angle from the coast road, past mini-markets, in the direction of the campsite. The village of Mírthios is situated up above on the slope right ahead. After 500m go right at a road junction and over a small bridge to reach the dilapidated campsite. Follow the field track along the west wall of the campsite to a house (3 mins.), cross a roadway and ascend an eroded path. After 5 mins. you come to a field track along which you can drive. Go straight on up towards the village ahead. Ancient gnarled olive trees in fantastic shapes line the path. You arrive at the village pump house and straight afterwards, below the first houses of **Mírthios**, you can go up right and come onto the through road of the village at the post office. Alternatively keep left and come to the village square and two tavernas where you can enjoy a refreshing drink and the beautiful view over the bay of Plakiás from the terrace.

View from Sellía to Plakiás bay.

32 Round walk near Mixórrouma

From Ano Mixórrouma through the Kíssanos river valley

Ano Mixórrouma – Fratí – Mixórrouma – Ano Mixórrouma

Starting point: Ano Mixórrouma, 300m, 3,5km before Spíli, on the main road Réthimnon – Spíli.
Walking time: village – Fratí ¾ hr., Fratí – Mixórrouma 1¼ hrs., Mixórrouma – Ano Mixórrouma ¼ hr.
Total time 2¼ hrs.
Difference in height: 250m.
Grade: easy walk, mainly on tarmac and gravel roads.
Stops and accommodation: tavernas in Ano Mixórrouma and Fratí, rooms for rent in Fratí, kafenia, hotels and rooms for rent in Spíli.
Bus services: Réthimnon – Spíli several times a day.
Tip: the nearby Spíli and its Venetian lion fountains.

The Kíssanos river whose source is in the Kédhros massif and is fed by the strong springs in Spíli, flows through several narrow valleys and gorges on its way south-west before reaching the sea in the well-known bay of Préveli. Just before Spíli, actually on the road, is situated the village of **Ano Mixórrouma** and a little below, hidden by a hill, the beautiful village of Mixórrouma which is slowly falling into disrepair. The latter is situated right by the river

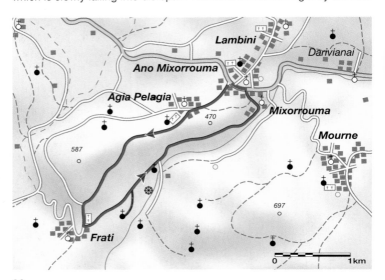

The old deserted village of Ano Mixórrouma.

which flows southwards through a densely overgrown green valley with beautiful situated churches.

At the western entrance to the village of **Ano Mixórrouma** a small tarmac road leads off right to Fratí. The 3.5km long stretch runs gently ascending a luxuriantly vegetated hill and soon allows you an open view of a steep dome-shaped hill where the village of **Fratí** lies at its foot. This small village provides tourists with a taverna in the square and a kafénion as well as accommodation in several rooms and studios.

If you leave the village again along the same road, follow a gravel road leading to the right after the last house, just before a small church. Shortly afterwards, at the next junction to the left continue at the same height into the valley. The roadway runs on the left-hand side of the valley and allows you beautiful views down to the luxuriant banks of the river. After about 1.6km the path leads downhill to the left at a junction to the bottom of the valley – to the right there's a short and pleasant detour in 15 minutes to two beautifully situated **chapels** above the river.

After walking for a total of one hour you will see a **bridge** on the right at another junction; stay on the left-hand side of the valley and walk upstream for a short way close to the overgrown bank of the Kíssanos river. The road ascends again for the last 15 minutes and brings you to the old village of **Mixórrouma**. A concrete path leads right at the first derelict house up to the old houses and to the still well-preserved church which stands between the ruins on its raised location with good views. Go straight on, following the telephone line, until you reach the connecting road again to Spíli.

33 From Asómatos to the palm beach of Préveli

A palm tree wood and old monasteries on the Libyan sea

Asómatos – palm beach – Moni Préveli

Starting point: Asómatos, 31km from Ré- thimnon in the direction of Plakiás.
Walking time: Asómatos – olive mill ½ hr., olive mill – Venetian bridge 20 mins., Ve- netian bridge – 2nd bridge ¼ hr., 2nd bridge – telegraph wire ¾ hr., telegraph wire – mouth of river ½ hr., ascent to the road 20 mins., road to Préveli monastery 20 mins., Préveli monastery – Gianioú 1 hr. Total time 4 hrs.
Difference in height: 250m.

Grade: easy but long walk. Water, sun protection necessary.
Stops and accommodation: tavernas and rooms in Plakiás, taverna with rooms in the bay 10 mins. east of the palm beach. Café in Asómatos.
Alternative: possible to walk on from the palm beach to Agios Pávlos (see Walk 34).
Bus services: Réthimnon – Asómatos – Plakiás – Préveli one to two a day.

Your route to the palm beach begins in **Asómatos** on the tarmac road in the direction of Réthimnon. After 800m before the tarmac road goes round a left-hand bend into the Kourtaliótiko gorge, take a sharp turn-off onto a de- scending concrete track which soon becomes a gravel path. Before that, though, you should make a detour to the **Agios Nikólaos chapel**. Continue along the road for a few hundred metres until concrete steps lead down to the chapel and the thundering springs of the Megalopótamos.

Back on the path to the palm beach walk straight on along the right-hand bank of the Megalopótamos (large river). The roadway ends before a small chapel. Continue straight on along the path, left past the chapel, and the vil- lage of Asómatos is directly ahead. After just 5 mins. you reach a closed- down **olive mill**. The year 1890 has been carved over the doorway. Follow a field path to the right and after 300m you will reach the broad tarmac road which goes from Lefkogía to the Préveli monastery. Reeds, myrtle bushes, plane trees and ivy line the banks of the Megalopótamos.

A little later you meet a delicate Venetian-looking **arch bridge** which was not built, however, until the 19th century. To the south you can see the ruins of the derelict monastery Káto Préveli, also called Mega Potámou, monas- tery of the big river.

Cross the river and walk along the gravel road on the left bank. After about an hour you come to **another arch bridge** with an inscription. Do not take any notice of the gravel road on the left (it goes eastwards from the palm beach bay) and follow the roadway branching off right above the river until you reach the derelict building of a small monastery of which only the cha- pel remains. Leave the gravel road to the right and go directly past the cha- pel. 25m after the chapel the path descends. Go left through a field and in

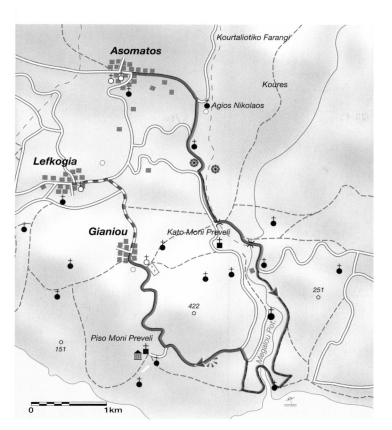

40 mins. on the other side there's a steep gravel road going down and then up again. Continue across the slope above the left bank. From the top you can see how the river is gradually being squeezed by the rock faces. The path slowly reaches the top and crosses over the top of the gorge walls. Go under a **telegraph wire**. 200m further on you can get your first glimpse of the estuary of the Megalopótamos river lined with palm trees. Shortly afterwards you can see the line of the coast running south into the distance. Then the path goes between boulders down to the estuary. In the bay on the left you can see a taverna which also rents rooms. The gravel road which

The Káto Préveli monastery at the entrance to the Kourtaliótiko gorge.

continued left at the second arched bridge finishes here. Many tourists come this far in their hire cars and then climb over to the **palm beach of Préveli** in 10 mins. After a good 2 hrs. walking you reach this beach, a naturally sheltered spot. You can walk up the valley for about half an hour to a narrow section of the river which is impassable.

For the next stage of the walk you have to wade across the side estuary of the river on a narrow strip of sand and climb up the rocks. After an ascent of 20 mins. you come to a gravel road and then a tarmac road which brings you further west to the **Préveli monastery**.

The 'monastery of Saint John Theologus' is enchanting with its unique position on the steep coast high above the Libyan Sea. It dates back to the 17th century and has been strongly influenced by the architectural style of the Venetians.

From the monastery there's a gravel path which zigzags over a col and down to the little village of **Gianioú**. The bus service is very limited here so you might possibly have to walk on further to Lefkogía.

The palm bay where the Megalopótamos river flows into the Libyan Sea.

34 From Agios Pávlos to Préveli bay

Rock formations and beaches

Agios Pávlos – Trí Pétres – Préveli bay

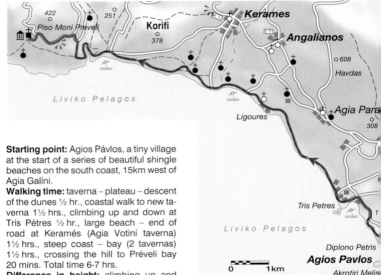

Starting point: Agios Pávlos, a tiny village at the start of a series of beautiful shingle beaches on the south coast, 15km west of Agia Galíni.

Walking time: taverna – plateau – descent of the dunes ½ hr., coastal walk to new taverna 1½ hrs., climbing up and down at Trís Pétres ½ hr., large beach – end of road at Keramés (Agia Votiní taverna) 1½ hrs., steep coast – bay (2 tavernas) 1½ hrs., crossing the hill to Préveli bay 20 mins. Total time 6-7 hrs.

Difference in height: climbing up and down four hills of up to 60m.

Grade: on the whole easy but strenuous coastal walk, mostly without paths over shingle and sand, some short, difficult and steep up and down climbing, rocky sections at times which you can walk round in the water. Good shoes necessary. No shade, not possible when seas are stormy!

Stops and accommodation: all tavernas mentioned offer rooms as well, several ta-

vernas with rooms in Agios Pávlos, hotels, b&b and tavernas in Agia Galíni and Plakiás.

Bus services: Réthimnon – Spíli – Agia Galíni several times a day, to Saktoúria once a day, Plakiás – Agia Galíni once a day, Préveli – Plakiás three times a day.

Boat services: Plakiás – Agia Galíni several times a week.

Agios Pávlos is not easy to reach and this is probably why there is little new building and few people on the beach. Either drive from Agia Galíni via Melambés (15km) and turn off left to Saktoúria to reach Agios Pávlos. Or take

Fantastic rock formations near Agios Pávlos.

the road from Spíli to Agia Galíni, turn off right after the little village of Nea Kria Vrise and after 15km reach Agios Pávlos via Saktoúria as above. The hamlet consists of two tavernas above the beach with rooms, a new block of apartments, further up another taverna with rooms and the little chapel of Agios Pávlos, built into the rocks. It is situated at the start of a unique series of beautiful shingle beaches with high sand dunes and fascinating rock formations all of which can be reached on foot. There are regular boat trips to Agios Pávlos from Agia Galíni especially in the summer.

From the **taverna** which is closest to the beach (good fish menu) there's a roadway leading down to the bay. A few metres after the end of the road a path goes over the steep sand dune, which is interspersed with rocks, and you cross a small **plateau**. Bordering the steep coast on the left there are some wonderful rock formations with multi-coloured zigzag patterns. From the edge of the plateau you can see down into the second bay. Walk above it and descend first over rocks, then on fine sand, down to the **sea** (½ hr. from the taverna). On descending into this second bay you have to wade knee deep round a rock projection (not possible in stormy seas).

You can stroll along by the sea for the next 1½ hrs. Shingle beaches, rock formations and high sand dunes form a fascinating backdrop. At first in a small bay which is enclosed by 50m high rocks (at this point there is no way through westwards) you have to turn away from the sea. A few metres above the beach there is a large **taverna**. Go past this on the road (it leads into Akoumia 12km away) to the top of the hill, then left westwards across

Top: the little church of Agios Pávlos on the south coast.
Right: three rocks (Trís Pétres) – the path goes above the steep coastline.

the narrow rocky peninsula, right at the edge of the slope, and climb down into the next bay. **Three rocks** (Trís Pétres) is the name of this tongue of land. Broad shingle beaches stretch from here to the west where you can already pick out Préveli bay and the monastery. A few newly built houses, 2 tavernas on the beach and many rooms for rent indicate the beginnings of a new development in this area.

After crossing a peninsula you reach a tarmac road (road from Kissou Kámbos to Keramés and further, to the coast) which ends just 10m from the water by the **taverna** of Agia Votiní.

From here keep walking along the narrow **strip of rocky coast** right beside by the sea (there's no alternative except up from the bays accessible by road). After the taverna, having crossed two bays with houses, a gravel road is being built directly parallel to the sea and which leads to the next large bay. After another 30 mins. you reach the wide bay at the estuary of the Megalopótamos. **Two tavernas** await you here. A gravel track connects the bay with the road between Moni Préveli and Plakiás. A distinct path takes you over the rocks in 20 mins. to **Préveli bay**. For the last stage of the walk to Préveli monastery, see Walk 33.

35 Onto Alp Trípiti

To the viewpoint over the Messará Plain and the Libyan Sea

Ano Méros – Kaloídhena – Alp Trípiti

Sheep looking for shade on the path to the Alp Trípiti.

Starting point: Ano Méros, 50km from Réthimnon, 30km from Timbáki.
Walking time: Ano Méros – Kaloídhena ¼ hr., Kaloídhena – Trípiti cave 1¾ hrs., cave – viewing point 20 mins. Total time 4½ hrs., including return.
Difference in height: 530m.
Grade: beautiful mountain walk on mostly marked paths. Good footwear. Take sufficient to drink.

Stops and accommodation: kafeníon in Ano Méros, rooms in Réthimnon or Agia Galíni.
Alternative: possible to climb up to the Kédhros summit from the Trípiti pasture, another 5 hrs. there and back. With your back to the Trípiti cave climb up without paths until you reach the summit.
Bus services: Réthimnon – Timbáki once a day.

The solitary rounded peak of Kédhros dominates to the west of Psilorítis. In between lies the Amári valley, practically cut off from the outside world. It is accessed on two roads. One runs along the western slopes of the Psilorítis and the other on the eastern flank of the Kédhros massif. The villages high up along the road profit from the good source of water in the area and there are still flowers blooming on the slopes of the Kédhros when everything else on Crete has dried up.

Begin your walk at the village church of **Ano Méros** and go along the main road from Réthimnon for about 150m. The Odos Markou Botsari leads downhill to the right, but you do not turn off until the next narrow street to the right and go up by the side of a water channel. At the first turn-off go left, then right and straight up. 5 mins. later turn right onto a roadway. Just after, a path turns off right and leads upwards over rushing spring water to the **chapel of Kaloídhena** ('I have seen well'). The newly renovated little church with a large rest area beneath plane trees, used to belong to a monastery which was destroyed during an uprising against the Turks in 1821. The name goes back to a miraculous vision.

Back on the roadway the ruins of an old water mill come straight into view. Continue up the roadway and keep left at a fork which soon follows. About 5 mins. after that turn right onto a field path (*red arrow*). You pass an iron gate and later the path crosses the roadway again. The *occasionally marked* path continues uphill until after ¾ hr. you meet the roadway once more. Go along for 60m then turn off left (*waymarkers*). Up ahead on the mountain ridge you aim for a right-angled gap. First of all follow a water pipe. After a concrete water channel by a plane tree a path zigzags uphill and is well marked. After about 2 hrs. you reach a **cave** on the **Alp Trípiti** with an iron gate and two barred windows. The cave is usually open and provides a good shelter as long as you can stand the smell of sheep dung.

Closeby there's a viewpoint. Standing with your back to the cave go up a gentle slope to the south-east. You have to clamber over several strips of rock and then climb up to a small plateau you can see ahead. Opposite in the south-east is the hill with a viewpoint (concrete pillar) from where there's a magnificent view over the Messará plain and the Libyan Sea.

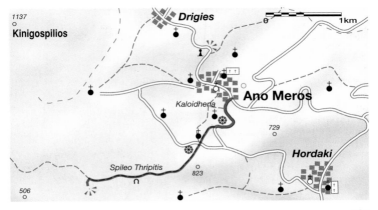

36 From Agia Galíni to Pitsídia

A relaxing beach walk along the Messará gulf

Agia Galíni – Kókkinos Pírgos – Kalamáki – Pitsídia

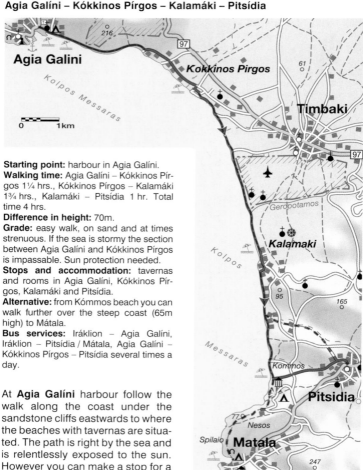

Starting point: harbour in Agia Galíni.
Walking time: Agia Galíni – Kókkinos Pírgos 1¼ hrs., Kókkinos Pírgos – Kalamáki 1¾ hrs., Kalamáki – Pitsídia 1 hr. Total time 4 hrs.
Difference in height: 70m.
Grade: easy walk, on sand and at times strenuous. If the sea is stormy the section between Agia Galíni and Kókkinos Pírgos is impassable. Sun protection needed.
Stops and accommodation: tavernas and rooms in Agia Galíni, Kókkinos Pírgos, Kalamáki and Pitsídia.
Alternative: from Kómmos beach you can walk further over the steep coast (65m high) to Mátala.
Bus services: Iráklion – Agia Galíni, Iráklion – Pitsídia / Mátala, Agia Galíni – Kókkinos Pírgos – Pitsídia several times a day.

At **Agia Galíni** harbour follow the walk along the coast under the sandstone cliffs eastwards to where the beaches with tavernas are situated. The path is right by the sea and is relentlessly exposed to the sun. However you can make a stop for a

The steep coast between Kómmos beach and Mátala.

swim at any time. After 10 mins. cross over the estuary to the Plátis river on a wobbly footbridge. 5 mins. later a nice walk goes along the gravel road just above the coastline. After 35 mins. the roadway finishes behind a ruin and you descend a gully to the sea. Do not go on to the wire mesh fence because the descent from there is dangerous! After 1¼ hrs. further along the shingle beach and past greenhouses you reach **Kókkinos Pírgos**. Now follow the road.

The best restaurant seems to be the Diónisos fish taverna where you can sit agreeably under tamarind trees on the beach. Kókkinos Pírgos is the start of an 8km long beach which stretches as far as Kómmos beach. It is one of the most beautiful and undeveloped beaches on Crete, thanks mainly to the military airport close by.

On the left-hand side of the harbour follow the promenade which ends after 10 mins. For the next 1½ hrs. you walk over sand and shingle beaches and later over stone slabs. Before **Kalamáki** there are some rocks about 30m high. A nice path to Pitsídia branches off from the bay behind these rocks. However, go on for another half an hour and your path up to Pitsídia begins at a hut with the sign *'Sea flights'*. The beach as far as the steep part of the coast is called **Kómmos beach** and is the local beach for **Pitsídia** which is situated just inland. It's half an hour from the beach into the village where you can find simple accommodation and tavernas.

You can also walk along the beach to **Mátala**. Continue above the steep coast from Kómmos beach then over the stone slabs which dropdown into the sea and are covered in mussels, starfish and sea urchins. Go on as far as Mátala rocks but you have to walk round them by going inland, because they are fenced off. You'll need shoes for this part of the walk.

37 Móni Odigítrias

Gorge walk to the Byzantine church of Agios Nikólaos on the coast

Móni Odigítrias – Agios Nikólaos – beach

Móni Odigítrias – a lovely well-cared for monastery that is worth a visit.

Starting point: Odigítrias monastery on the Messará plain, turn off to Sívas before Pitsídia on the road to Mátala, continue to Listarós and drive 4km along the gravel road to the monastery.
Walking time: monastery – junction ¾ hr., junction – start of the gorge ¾ hr., gorge – church / bay ½ hr. Total time 4½-5 hrs. including return.
Difference in height: 300m.
Grade: easy walk, partly on gravel roads, partly in the stony riverbed, little shade, easy route finding.

Stops and accommodation: in the villages of the Messará plain, many rooms and tavernas near to Mátala, large choice in Mátala and Míres.
Bus services: Iráklion – Mátala several times a day, bus stop at the junction to Sívas, closer access is only possible by car.
Tip: the Messará plain offers several archaeological sights in close proximity – Festós, Agia Triáda, Agii Déka, Górtys. Even Mátala is worth a visit out of the tourist season.

The **Odigítrias monastery**, perched on a rounded hilltop at a height of 275m with magnificent views and made safe on three sides by steep rocky terrain, is the starting point for this walk. You drive to it from the Messará plain via the villages of Sívas and Listarós (from here a good 4km of gravel road), which radiate peaceful simplicity in contrast to the noise and bustle near Mátala. The large well-cared for monastery is inhabited only by one monk and his mother. They both spend their time renovating and caring for this large property.
NB: to go inside, visitors must be properly dressed, women wearing a dress or a skirt, and men with long trousers.

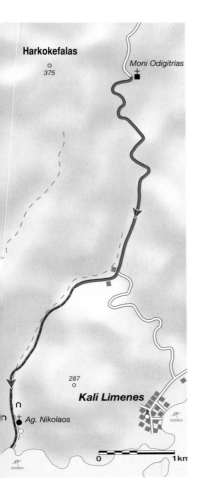

The gravel road winds down from the monastery on the hill in the direction of Kalí Liménes. After 3km, behind some sheep and goat sheds on the right-hand side (after the last fenced agricultural property), a broad **gravel road** swings right into a deep river valley. Drive to this point if you have your own vehicle. The increasingly deteriorating road leads down into the valley and goes southwards near to or actually in the riverbed itself. The road ends near some **sheds** with fenced-off pastureland on the right-hand side of the river. The valley is enclosed on both sides by yellow sandstone formations which gradually move closer and closer to one another. A narrow footpath now follows the course of the stream which only runs with a little water in winter, but is densely overgrown with oleander bushes. After about ½ hr. steeper limestone formations replace the sandstone. The valley narrows into a **gorge**. 20 mins. later you find yourself right in the middle of the narrow gorge, with caves and huge reddish cliffs on both sides. Walk through the gorge for another ¼ hr. until you see the well-preserved Byzantine **church of Saint Antonios** on the left built close to the rock face (a cistern at the entrance). After the church the gorge opens out into an enormous almost spherical valley basin, the rock faces become lower and a beautiful shingle bay enclosed by rocks is your objective. This idyllic **bay** is only accessible on foot or by boat, but is nevertheless very busy in summer.

The White Mountains

The village of Lákki with a backdrop of Léfka Óri.

The biggest and most compact range of mountains on Crete has the distinction of having most of the island's highest mountains (40 summits over 2000m) concentrated here. Most of the huts of the EOS (Haniá section) are also here: the Kallérgi hut above Omalós, the Volika hut in the north (accessible from Kámbi) and the new Távri hut under the **Kástro massif** east of the White Mountains. In winter this is the only area completely covered in snow from a height of 1000m upwards (often for weeks on end). There are even ski runs for those experienced enough. And last of all, this mountain area of Crete is the biggest provider of water. It feeds not only the few rivers on the island which are running the whole year round, but also the abundant and fulsome springs down as far as the south coast.

Cutting deep into these mountains is one of the longest gorges in Europe, the **Samariá gorge**, a unique natural phenomenon and the biggest tourist attraction on the island. It is the natural habitat and reserve for many rare species of plants and trees, plus the kri-kri, the wild goat which is threatened with extinction. Crete's only **National Park**, established in 1962, is supposed to protect this natural monument, but it has at the same time become a magnet for thousands of visitors each day. Just as impressive and usually more demanding, are other **beautiful gorges** which can also be walked from the White Mountains down to the south, such as the Agia Iríni, the Arádhena, the Anópolis and the Imbros gorges, to name but a few.

There are many beautifully located villages around the edge of the White Mountains. Until recently untouched by tourism, the traditions and characteristic features of these Cretans have been preserved more strongly (especially in **Sfakiá**, the south-eastern part).

The White Mountains offer the ambitious walker very long and strenuous mountain hikes, for example the ascent of some high peaks from the Omalós plain, or the ascent of the **Kástro** (a long day trip). The **Omalós plain** in the west and the **Askífou plain** in the east are ideal starting points for the finest and most demanding mountain walks.

Walks in the high regions of western Crete, particularly during the very hot summers, are a welcome change from a pure beach holiday. Families offer friendly accommodation and a good traditional cuisine in the small villages.

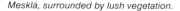

Mesklá, surrounded by lush vegetation.

38 From Thérisso to Mesklá

Mountain villages at the foot of the White Mountains

Thérisso – Zoúrva – Mesklá

Starting point: southern end of Thérisso, 550m. The village lies at the end of the Thérissiano gorge, 14km south of Haniá, and is the birthplace of Venizelos.
Walking time: Thérisso – Zoúrva 1¼ hrs., Zoúrva – Mesklá 1 hr.
Total time 2¼ hrs.
Difference in height: ascent 200m, des-

cent 500m.
Grade: easy walk and pleasant descent on gravel road.
Stops and accommodation: kafenía in Thérisso, Zoúrva (simple cooking) and Mesklá. Hotels and campsites in Haniá.
Bus services: Haniá – Thérisso 7.30, Mesklá – Haniá 14.30 (weekdays).

Thérisso is of special significance to the Cretans. This village is the birth-place of Eleftherios Venizelos, the independence fighter and national hero of Crete and one of Greece's greatest statesmen. To reach Thérisso take the main road at the south-western edge of Haniá to Perivólia / Thérisso. The road soon squeezes its way through the gorge shaded with plane trees. The village of Thérisso, surrounded by lush greenery, lies at a height of 550m, with a backdrop of the White Mountains, covered with snow in spring. It also lies at the end of one of the most beautiful gorges in Crete, which, with its almost vertical walls, makes a rewarding objective for a walk.

Mesklá church.

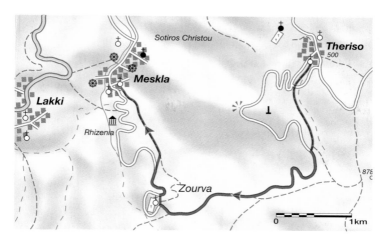

Leave Thérisso at its southern end by the old double-aisled **Agia Aikateríni church** situated under an enormous plane tree. 20m behind it (at the place-name sign) a footpath turns off left which goes along the river. After 10 mins. you come to a roadway which crosses over the stream on a bridge. However, keep right and go through a wire fence and uphill along the right of a stream.

The path gradually goes away from the stream and after 35 mins. divides into two by some oleander bushes. Stay on the higher path on the right until you reach a wired-off sheep pen and above it continue straight over the **gravel road** which crosses the path. In the distance you can see the village of Lákki with its large blue church dome. At the left end of the nearest mountain ridge you can see **Zoúrva**. Take the gravel road to Zoúrva which goes below a high rock face shaded by cypress trees. A kafeníon with a pleasant terrace offers a place to sit and rest and take a look at the well-preserved wood-fired oven.

After that continue on the road through the village and along the tarmac road past the cemetery. 20 mins. after leaving Zoúrva a shortcut turns off steeply up to the right (*waymarked*). 5 mins. later follow a gravel path which joins another shortly after a right-hand bend. Continue down this to the left. After 20 mins. it rejoins the roadway which comes from Zoúrva and goes on to Mesklá. After the first house of **Mesklá** a path takes a shortcut to the left into the village.

Soon you are surrounded with the sound of rushing water (orange groves). 400m after a bridge you come to two kafenía and the bus stop.

39 From Kámbi to the Vólika hut, 1260m

Into the White Mountains from the north

Kámbi – Vólika hut – Kámbi

Shepherds' stone shelter on the way up to into the White Mountains.

Starting point: church (bus stop) in Kámbi, 25km from Haniá.
Walking time: Kámbi – cleft in the rock 1¼ hrs., cleft – gorge descent 1¼ hrs., gorge descent – Vólika hut 1 hr., descent 2½ hrs. Total time 6 hrs.
Difference in height: 670m.
Grade: waymarkers in places. Fitness and

some sense of direction required. Good footwear. Take sufficient water.
Stops and accommodation: two kafenía in Kámbi.
Hotels and campsites in Haniá.
Alternative: from the hut ascend Mávri, 2069m, or Spáthi, 2046m.
Bus services: from Haniá.

The starting point is the **church** in the village square where the bus stops too. If you stand in front of the church you will see behind the kafeníon a steep wooded side of a gorge in the distance. Your objective, the Vólika hut, is just above the tops of the trees. Go right on the gravel road past the kafeníon southwards towards the mountains. Turn right at a fork in the road after a small kafeníon and by a wayside shrine. At the next fork go between two olive trees to reach the houses at the southern end of Kámbi. At these houses go immediately right and then left at the next fork past a vineyard. After half an hour you reach a **shed**. Take the path in front steeply up left. Once at the top of the hill you can see the highest peaks behind the gorge-like cleft. On the right is a high wooded dome-shaped mountain. Continue in this direction (occasional *cairns*) and then directly towards the gorge-like cleft again. A broad path goes down and across a U-shaped valley. As you start going uphill again you will see EOS written in red on a rock.

The path is more frequently marked now whereas the signs in the later stages are usually often difficult to see. Go past a small pile of stones and through the rocky wasteland. Then continue along the right-hand edge of the gorge. Later cross the gorge where the path is just sufficiently visible. The gorge divides into two further up and you ascend the left **gully**. You will soon discover a small geological wonder where the rock is layered like puff pastry. It's now a comfortable stroll over stone slabs up to the **Vólika hut** at 1260m. At weekends you will often find the hut open as it's a popular destination for members of Haniá's mountaineering club. Water is only available in the hut.

The hut is an ideal starting point for the ascent of the northern two-thousander of the White Mountains. A good sense of direction and some alpine experience are absolutely essential for these walks. You need 2 hrs. to the summit of Mávri, 2069m, as well as for Spáthi, 2046m, and a bit longer up to the Agia Pnévma, 2254m, and the Griás Sorós, 2231m.

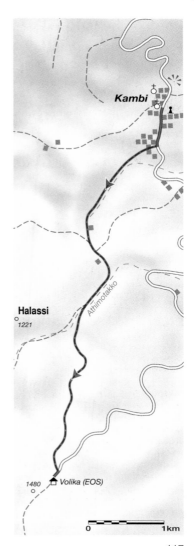

40 Descent from Omalós plain

From the White Mountains into the Agia Iríni gorge

Omalós – Agios Theodóri – Agia Iríni gorge

Starting point: Omalós 1050m, 36km from Haniá.

Walking times: Omalós – Agios Theodóri ¾ hrs., Agios Theodóri – junction ½ hr., junction – Agia Iríni gorge 1¼ hrs. Total time 2½ hrs.

Difference in height: ascent 100m, descent 600m.

Grade: easy walk, at first along gravel and tarmac roads, easy route finding. Possible all year round. After lengthy periods of rain the walk through the gorge is not possible, so descend instead into the village of Agia Iríni.

Stops and accommodation: tavernas and rooms for rent in Omalós, tavernas at the entrance to the Agia Iríni gorge during the season.

Bus connections: three times daily Haniá – Omalós from May to October, daily Haniá – Soúgia all year round (bus stop at the entrance to the gorge).

After the last houses of Omalós a dirt and gravel road branches off to the right from the road in the direction of the Samariá gorge. It leads in a wide bend along the western edge of the plateau. After 3km you reach the newly built tarmac road between Omalós and the road from Haniá to Soúgia. Going uphill continue for about another 500m along the road out over the western edge of the plateau. On the left-hand side after the little church of **Agios Theodóri** at a large car park, the newly constructed hiking trail begins down to the village of Agia Iríni or directly into the **Agia Iríni** gorge.

The route goes along an old bridle path which has been in use since the Venetian and Turkish occupations of Crete. Fairly short sections are still well-preserved and are some of the most beautiful parts of this trail.

The path, narrow at first, descends over the right-hand hillside at the start of the valley sometimes beneath large pine trees. After a few minutes you then walk downhill along the old paved bridle path.

The old path was destroyed in places when the road above was being built and has consequently been newly laid. From here there are beautiful views of the upper regions of the White Mountains, across the south-western wooded mountains at the edge of the Léfka Óri and down into the deep cleft of the Agia Iríni gorge. About 30 mins. after you have negotiated the last steep slope along the paved bridle path round regular hairpin bends you come to a **junction** in a small level valley. The bridle path runs straight on, for the most part well-preserved, in about 45 mins. down to the village of **Agia Iríni**. It leads finally across an old stone arch bridge at the southern end of the village and meets the hiking trail (Walk 21) at the entrance to the gorge near the new taverna.

Your route, on the other hand, follows the newly laid narrow footpath which brings you down into the increasingly steep valley in a south-westerly direction. On the right-hand side of the valley it first descends across open hillsides on increasingly steep terrain. Sections of rock on both sides and solitary standing trees indicate the Agia Iríni gorge. Continue round some narrow zigzags where boulders and ledges can often be avoided down steps. After a good hour's descent down the path from the junction you come to the bottom of the **Agia Iríni gorge** in a dense mixed wood. Finally go past

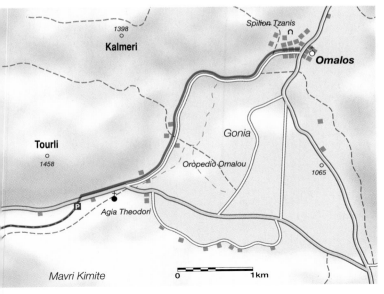

the ruins of houses and cisterns and directly by the stream you meet the well-extended gorge path from Agia Iríni to Soúgia. An information board tells you that there used to be an old partisan hide-out at the ruins in the time of the Turkish occupation. The strategically well-placed location enabled them to quickly reach the south coast from the mountains. You can now go up along beside the stream to the start of the gorge at the village of Agia Iríni in just under 30 minutes or decide to walk another 4 hours through the Agia Iríni gorge and reach the south coast at Soúgia (see Walk 21).

Right: through the Agia Iríni gorge.
Below: the Omalós plain in the White Mountains.

41 From Omalós to the Kallérgi hut, 1677m, and to Melindaoú, 2133m

At the heart of the White Mountains

Xylóskalo – Kallérgi hut – Psári – Mávri – Melindaoú

Starting point: Xylóskalo, 1300m, at the upper edge of the Omalós plain, right by the car park at the entrance to the Samariá gorge, where the gravel road turns off left to the Kallérgi hut (signposted).

Walking time: Xylóskalo – Kallérgi hut 1 hr., Kallérgi hut – Shepherds' saddle 50 mins., Shepherds' saddle – Psári 1 hr., Psári – Mávri ½ hr., Mávri – Melindaoú ¾ hr., return to Xylóskalo 3 hrs. Total time 7 hrs.

Difference in height: 1000m.

Grade: easy, but tiring mountain walk;

half can be done on gravel road, otherwise narrow mountain path (with waymarkers).

Good footwear. No shade. No drinking water on the way.

Stops and accommodation: b&b and hotel in Omalós, Kallérgi hut accommodation (telephone inquiry necessary, tel: 0821/74560), taverna and kiosk in Xylóskalo.

Bus services: Haniá – Omalós several a day, (May to October), last bus from Xylóskalo to Haniá at 16.00.

From the upper edge of **Omalós plain**, about 1km before the car park, a gravel track goes left and zigzags steeply up to the **Kallérgi hut**, 1677m. The hut, built and run in the style of an alpine hut, stands behind a ridge with an open view down into the Samariá gorge and up onto Gíngilos and Volakías opposite. You need a good hour for this ascent. Shorter and nicer, however, is the **footpath** to the hut which will take you just under an hour (just before the entrance to the gorge, go up left across the hill – only the second half of the route is on the road).

From the **hut** follow the gravel road again to the east. It winds up through the barren hills and in just under an hour reaches the **Shepherds' saddle** below the Psári mountain. There's a large brown *sign* in Greek lettering indicating the ascent route and the distinct red and white waymarkings start a little further on. There are hardly any

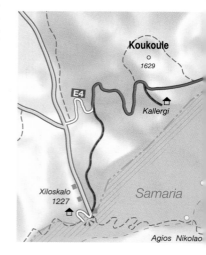

View across the deep ravine of the Samariá gorge towards Melindaoú.

paths across this open terrain. The landscape is characterised by gravely hills, stones and larger rocks with scanty vegetation. But you are compensated with a constantly changing outlook, either northwards to the coast or westwards over the Samariá gorge to the range of mountains opposite. You

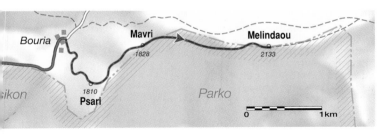

reach the top of **Psári** in just under an hour. After another 30 mins. over the ridge you come to the neighbouring summit of **Mávri**. A gentle descent follows into the next hollow. Ignore a summit on your left and follow the yellow waymarkings over the ridge to the summit of **Melindaoú**, 2135m high. Not until now could you see the other peaks of the still higher summit of Pahnés mountain. An imposing landscape – only scree, rocks and conical mountains and not a sound to be heard. Return on the same path to the Kallérgi hut and down the road to Omalós.

42 From Omalòs to the Koukoúle

Above the Omalós plateau

Omalós – Kallérgi – Koukoúle – chain of hills – Omalós

Starting point: Omalós, 1050m, 36km away from Haniá.
Walking times: Omalós – gravel road turn-off ¾ hrs., turn-off – Kallérgi hut 1½ hrs., Kallérgi hut – Koukoúle ¼ hr., Koukoúle – 1580m point 1 hr., 1580m point – gravel road (descent) 1½ hrs., gravel road – Omalós ½ hr. Total time 5½ hrs., but only 4½ hrs. if you drive as far as Xylóskalo.
Difference in height: 700m.
Grade: moderate walk. Tarmac and gravel roads at the start, otherwise without paths, a lot of scree. In poor visibility route finding over terrain without paths is very difficult from the Kallérgi hut onwards. Walking poles are recommended for the rather long and tiresome descent where there are no paths. Only possible if there's no snow (around May to November).
Stops and accommodation: tavernas/

rooms for rent in Omalós, taverna / kiosque at the entrance to the Samariá gorge (in the season), overnight stop / food in the Kallérgi hut (book in advance, tel: 08210/74560, staffed May to October).
Bus connections: Haniá – Omalós three times a day May to October, Haniá – Soúgia daily all year round (bus stop at the entrance to the gorge).

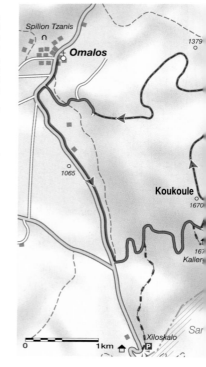

This walk, at first deceptively easy, then strenuous, offers you some impressive views of the Léfka Óri mountains and the beautiful views down onto the Omalós plain, but you must be able to make a safe descent on steep terrain without paths; sturdy hiking boots are essential. From **Omalós** it's a gentle ascent, following the tarmac road for 45 minutes to the top (southern) edge of the flat plain. 1km before the end of the road at an E4 sign and a signpost to the Kallérgi hut, follow the gravel road to the left (east) which zigzags up to the col before the **Kallérgi hut** (see Walk 41). The Kallérgi hut (1680m) is an ideal resting place before the walk across the chain of hills and before the descent to the plain. Across from the hut there's an extensive and spectacular view of the deep cleft of the Samariá gorge and its side valleys, as well as the massifs of Gíngilos, Volakiás and Pachnés. With Koukoúle (1670m) a chain of hills begins north of the hut which forms the eastern edge of the Omalós plain. Walk along tracks and goat paths without any great variation in height above the Omalós plain with wonderful views down onto the plain and the Léfka Óri mountain chain.

From the Kallérgi hut go the short way back to the col and continue along the gravel road in the direction of the shepherds' col.

The summit of Volakías.

After about 200m turn off left and ascend the first hill, Koukoúle (1670m); a concrete pillar marks this trig point. Follow the ridge to the north along some sheep tracks. The path leads directly along the crest of the ridge, sometimes right, sometimes left a few metres below. A short ascent brings you to the next hilltop (1660m); from here go north-westwards and there's a view down to the wide oval of the Omalós plain. Keep walking along the prominent flat ridge which lies next to the Omalós plain. After about an hour from Koukoúle you come to the last flat hill (1580m) at a cairn; you are already at the height of the little village of Omalós which lies on the left (west) 500m further below. Descend the strenuous western slope without paths; gravel, fairly large boulders and bizarre rhizomes are all you can see. Steeper and rocky places can be circumvented. A valley begins further below, partly wooded, partly covered in gravel. Continue descending at the left-hand edge, always heading for a gravel road which ends below the hill at a field. Orientate yourself towards the end of this gravel road which is your objective.

The descent leads partly beneath large cypress trees, past an enormous lightly bleached, dead tree, sometimes through dense undergrowth and marvellous flowers. It is not until the last 100 vertical metres that the going gets a bit easier. The gravel road leads out onto the plain round a wide left-hand bend and reaches the tarmac road just before the first houses of Omalós.

43 To Gíngilos, 2080m, and Volakías, 2126m

Two-thousanders above the Samariá gorge

Xylóskalo – Gíngilos – Volakías

Starting point: Xylóskalo, 1300m, the upper edge and the southernmost point of the Omalós plain. If you do not come by bus or car, allow about three quarters of an hour to walk along the road from Omalós over the plain.

Walking time: car park – spring 1½ hrs., spring – col ½ hr., col – summit of Gíngilos 1¼ hrs., Gíngilos – summit of Volakías 1¼ hr. Total time 6½ hrs. (Gíngilos), or 9 hrs. (Volakías).

Difference in height: Gíngilos 850m, Volakías 150m (total 1000m).

Grade: moderately difficult mountain climb, partly on rocky ground, surefootedness and a good head for heights necessary, extensive snowfields often cover the many holes and limestone caves in spring when there's a danger of snow-collapse.

Stops and accommodation: see Walk 41.

Bus services: see Walk 41.

The Omalós plain is an ideal starting point for a whole series of hikes in the White Mountains and there are many opportunities for staying overnight, in particular the small well-run Hotel Neos Omalós open all year round.

The walk up begins at the **car park** right by the entrance to the Samariá gorge, past the former **Xénia** hut which is no longer allowed to offer overnight stops because it's on National Park land. Go directly past the front door where there's a spectacular view from the terrace and a path goes up the steep slope to the left at a sign indicating the spring above. Follow the well-constructed path which zigzags up the steep mountain ridge. After about 30 mins. the path descends gently into the side valley coming from the Samariá gorge. This scenery is amazingly like the high alpine areas in mainland Europe with its many large old pine trees, bizarre root structures and dramatic rock formations. You will be repeatedly impressed with the breath-taking views across the Samariá gorge way below to the mountains opposite, Pahnés and a few other two-thousanders. Continue through a huge rock arch into the gorge below. In just over an hour you reach the **spring** which pours out of the rock at a height of 1700m and reliably provides the

The broad ridge of Gíngilos. Volakías on the left.

walker with deliciously clear water all year round. From the spring a narrow path zigzags up to the **col** between Psiláfi and Gíngilos, 1850m. From here there's a splendid view across the Trípiti gorge to the Libyan Sea. The path now goes up the steep rocky slope past a deep 150m vertical hole (made safe with a handrail). For this part of the walk you need to be surefooted and have a good head for heights as there are some steep sections needing the use of hands for balance. *Cairns* and *red waymarkers* lead you up the mainly firm rock path until you reach the flattened area where a pyramid of stones marks the summit of **Gíngilos**. From here there's a tremendous panorama – Haniá in the north with its coastal region, the almost circular Omalós plain below, the White Mountains in the east and the islands of Gávdos and Gavdopoúla in the south.

A short descent on gravel, a traverse and then another 150m ascent and you find yourself on the second summit, **Volakías**, 2126m. Take your time to enjoy the spectacular view.

For the return cross the south slope of Gíngilos just below the summit and shortly before the steep section you rejoin your ascent path which brings you back to the starting point.

44 Samariá gorge

In Crete's National Park

Xylóskalo – Agios Nikólaos – Samariá – Agia Rouméli

Starting point: Xylóskalo, the upper edge and at the same time the most southern point of the Omalós plain, at the end of the road from Haniá 43km away.

Walking time: Xylóskalo – Agios Nikólaos 1½ hrs., Agios Nikólaos – Samariá 1 hr., Samariá – Agia Rouméli 2½ hrs. Total time 5 hrs.

Differene in height: descent 1300m.

Grade: easy, but long and strenuous gorge walk with good paths. Stream crossings in the lower part, level of water even higher in May in particular. Good footwear necessary even in safe dry weather due to the many dusty polished stone steps. Entrance fee of 3,52 Euros.

Stops and accommodation: many tavernas and rooms in Haniá, Omalós and Agia Rouméli. A kiosk and taverna in Xylóskalo, but nowhere to stay overnight.

Bus services: Haniá – Omalós three times a day from May to October.

Boat connections: Agia Rouméli – Hóra Sfakíon several times a day.

The descent of the Samariá gorge is the best-known and most popular walk in Crete. From a height of 1300m you descend about 16km from the high mountains into the incomparably beautiful mountain valley and walk through the narrow gorge sections in the middle until finally the valley opens out towards the sea. No greater contrasts are possible even on this island.

Unfortunately the affects of mass tourism are evident even in this particularly magnificent region which is greatly in need of protection. Busload after

busload of people pour into the gorge from above. Shouting, taking photos, armed with video cameras they rush through the gorge making it impossible to linger and take in the surroundings. A lot of tourists turn back after a few minutes or at the latest after an hour so that the middle part of the gorge is relatively peaceful. But then there are just as many hoards of tourists coming up from the sea to the narrowest section causing congestion again in the final part of the walk. In any case it's worth making a start as early as possible.

At first the path goes down hundreds of steep steps. The 1000m rock face of Gíngilos towers up on the right-hand side of the valley. It's a well-constructed path and there's a handrail wherever necessary. Extensive repairs are required every year since rain and snow often cause complete devastation. During winter (October to May) the gorge is closed anyway and the entrance guarded due to considerable rock fall which makes the path dangerous. This is true of most of the gorges in Crete. After the little church of **Agios Nikólaos** the path runs close to the riverbed. The richness of tree and alpine plant species, the large boulders and many springs conjure up the magic of this valley. The path leads to the former settlement of Samariá mostly in the shade of large pine and cypress trees. A basin-shaped valley opens out and from here you can see up to the huge mountains of Pahnés and Volakías. The old village of **Sama-**

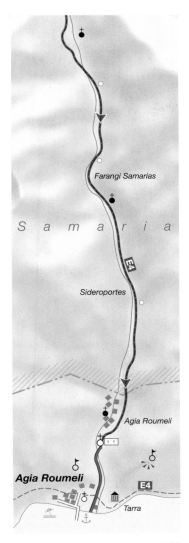

Arched bridge at the old village of Agia Rouméli.

riá, which you reach after 3 hrs. of walking, lies at a relatively narrow part in the valley so that it has little sunlight in the afternoon. A few of the old houses have been renovated and serve now as First Aid posts, information huts and accommodation for the National Park workers. Now the valley is becoming more and more narrow, the walls, at times overhanging for more than 300m, before you reach the **Sideropórtes** (iron gates). At only 3m wide this is the narrowest part of the gorge. Suddenly, after passing the narrowest point, you walk out into the first sunshine for hours and feel the heat of the south coast.

You reach the National Park border in the **old village of Agia Rouméli**. The tourist routine gets under way again at the entrance where your tickets are checked, since staying overnight in the gorge is not allowed. Half a dozen hastily erected kiosks offer everything that you might have missed in those few hours. Mountains of rubbish are heaped up right next to the edge of the path. Now continue through the ruins of the old village to the new village of **Agia Rouméli** which was built directly on the shingle beach. Here weary visitors are taken in and fed until they continue their journey by ferry.

It's recommended that you stay here until the next day at least, for the evening hours bring an unusual peace and tranquillity allowing you to absorb the century-long isolation of this village.

The new village of Agai Rouméli lies at the end of the Samariá gorge.

45 To the summit of Kástro, 2218m

From Amoudári via the Távri hut up to Kástro

Amoudári – Távri hut – Kástro

Starting point: Amoudári, 740m, on the Askífou plain, on the road between Vrísses and Hóra Sfakíon.
Walking time: Amoudári – Távri hut 2 hrs., Távri hut – end of the road 1 hr., ascent over the north-east ridge 2½ hrs., descent over the south-east ridge 2 hrs., return from the second plateau 2 hrs.
Total time 9½ hrs.
Difference in height: 1500m.
Grade: moderate, at times exhausting and strenuous mountain walk. For the

most part without paths and requiring surefootedness. Sturdy hiking or mountain boots necessary for the sharp-edged boulders and many slabs. Care and attention needed on the stretches of old snow in the higher regions covering many deep holes in the rock and crevasses.
Stops and accommodation: rooms and tavernas in Amoudári, Vrísses and Hóra Sfakíon.
Bus services: Haniá – Hóra Sfakíon via Vrísses and return several times a day.

The ascent of Kástro, the most eastern of the two-thousanders in the White Mountains, requires stamina, surefootedness, good route-finding ability and settled weather. It's a long day's walk and there's little opportunity for shelter. Thunderstorms in Crete are possible right into the summer and even in autumn. They build up quickly and tend to be more violent and dangerous than in mainland Europe.

The 740m high village of **Amoudári** serves as the starting point for this mountain walk. From the main road to Hóra Sfakíon a road branches off right to the church. The road goes uphill past the church, then past a dairy, winding steeply up to the first plateau. On the first narrow left-hand bend 100m after the dairy, go straight on following the old path up the hill past a big new cistern, left past a sheepfold and into the wood uphill. After about half an hour you cross the **gravel road** and then follow the old footpath again on the other side (from here *E4 waymarkings*). A little further on, but easier to find: at the second bend go along a gravel track which leads to a newer sheepfold. Well-marked with cairns. The path zigzags up through a thin mountain forest of pines and oak

The Askífou plain, Amoudári in the background.

trees to the edge of the first plateau at a height of 1,150m. Going gently downhill you come to some flat agricultural land and meet the gravel road again. Follow this to the left and after a wide bend there's a turn-off. 500m

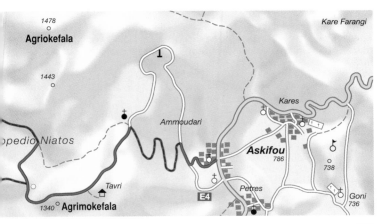

along left is the **Távri hut** belonging to the Haniá section of the EOS. The path now goes in a big loop to the right onto the second plateau which at 1240m is almost circular and totally flat. At the start of this plain on the right there's a large cistern, 30m away from the road. From here you also have a clear view of the rest of your route. The road goes in a wide bend round the outside of the plain. You cross the plain and keep to the right-hand (northern) edge. The two **ridges** coming down to the east which finish on the plain are your ascent and descent routes. At the upper edge of the plain you meet the roadway again. Follow this to the **end** (1 hr. from the EOS hut). Now you find yourself on the old path again which leads over a small col and descends gradually to an old cistern in the shade of some large trees. Just before follow the clearly visible E4 posts up left. Climb for a good half an hour over sharp-edged rock, stone slabs and through dense undergrowth until at a height of 1500m a wide **basin-shaped valley** opens up. The ridge forms the border to the valley on the right hand side and goes up to the top of the Kástro massif, which consists of three peaks of the same height, the left hand one being the summit point. Follow the E4 markings right along the ridge itself to the top. At a height of 1,950m the E4 turns off to the west. Clamber left over the stone slabs and rocks of the first peak and after a short descent reach a hollow where you'll find snow until late spring. Continue past the second peak and over sheer boulders climb the steep ridge which leads up to the summit plateau of **Kástro**. The ascent has taken 2½ hrs. You can now enjoy the view to the north and south coasts with the many villages, the Askífou plain way below and the endless rock formations and peaks of the White Mountains.

The descent route goes down eastwards over the broad ridge, gradually at first and then there's a short steep section which ends in a completely level **ridge area**. Before it drops down steeply eastwards to the second plateau go across right into the shallow **hollow** below. Follow the cleft in the valley towards the big plain and climb down over stone slabs relatively steeply through a mass of limestone subsidence and sharp edged rocks into the little side valley and follow this out onto the **plain**. 2 hrs. of strenuous descent are behind you and now there's another 1½ to 2 hrs. of fairly comfortable walking on the same path back to Amoudári.

The road ends at the second plateau.

The Ida Massif

Psilorítis (2456m) from the south.

The Ida massif which lies in the eastern part of the **Réthimnon** district, is steeped in century-old Cretan mythology. Young Zeus was hidden high up in a cave (Ideon Andron) and grew up in the care of the shouting Kuretes. In the Kamáres cave on the south slopes of the mountain range valuable pottery was excavated and gave the name to the period of Minoan art. Those who have stood on the highest summit of these mountains can experience an uplifting feeling when the blue of the sky blends with the sun, and land and sea blur into one below.

The highest mountain of this limestone range is **Psilorítis** with a height of 2456m, only 3m higher than the highest point of the White Mountains. The chapel of Tímios Stavrós marks the summit. In winter the upper regions are deep in snow, but it does not stay as long as in the White Mountains. The development of a ski resort is being considered in spite of this. Although the scenery is not as dramatic as in the White Mountains, some of the gorges are almost as impenetrable and animals in danger of extinction and birds such as the lammergeier and griffon vulture, are under protection.

On the northern slopes many villages are sustained by the abundance of springs in the mountains. The main source of income of the inhabitants is the rearing of sheep and goats for the production of milk, meat and wool. Amongst the many villages **Margarítes** has become an attraction with its pottery. Also the weavers village of **Anógia** has become a tourist magnet, partly due to the fact that you can drive from there along a 21km road up to the almost circular Nídha plain, 1370m, and the **Ideon Andron cave**. The shortest route onto the top of Psilorítis begins from there. At the north-eastern foot of the Psilorítis, only 23km from Réthimnon, is the Arkádi monastery which has become a national memorial for its heroic resistance to the Turks. The massif suddenly loses height in the west and is bounded almost completely by the Amári basin. Zarós, one of the villages in the southern foothills, has become well-known for its abundant springs. Trout is successfully farmed here, but there's also a beautiful walk up the gorge into the mountains. The southern foothills of the Ida are eventually lost in the largest agricultural area of the island, the fertile **Messará plain**. The border between eastern and western Crete is marked by the road from Iráklion to Agii Déka.

Shepherds' stone shelters above the Nídha plain.

46 To the summit of Psilorítis, 2456m

From the Nídha plain up to Tímios Stavrós, the highest summit on Crete

Nídha – Alp Kóllita – Psilorítis

Starting point: pavilion on the Nídha plain, 21km from Anógia.

Walking time: Nídha – Alp Kóllita 1¾ hrs., Alp Kóllita – north-western ascent 1½ hrs., traversing the summit ¾ hr. Total time 7 hrs. there and back.

Difference in height: 1200m.

Grade: elevated walk, easily visible E4 waymarkers, only in stable weather and with the necessary equipment. Take sufficient to drink. Surefootedness and experience required in the event of snowfields.

Stops and accommodation: taverna at the starting point, tavernas and rooms in Anógia.

Alternative: possible descent from the summit via the EOS mountain hut to Fourfourás (E4) or Kouroútes (Amári basin).

Bus services: Réthimnon – Anógia twice a day. Iráklion – Anógia six times a day.

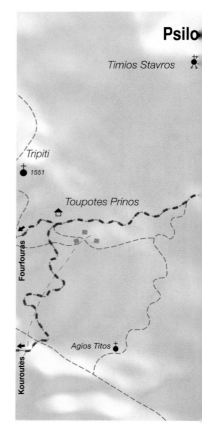

This walk deals with the shortest ascent of the summit of Psilorítis. The road from Anógia takes you already onto a hill of almost 1500m. It ends below the Ideon Cave (Ideon Andron), where the child Zeus grew up and was kept hidden from Kronos, his revengeful father. The excavations in the cave in 1884 were under the direction of the archaeologist, E. Fabricius.

In 1955, during further excavations, valuable pottery and bronze objects were discovered. The Greek archaeologist, Jannis Sakellarakis, has had the floor of the cave systematically sifted through in the last few years in the hope of uncovering more. The cave has unfortunately remained closed to the public in this time. The items found during excavation are on display in the Archaeological Museum in Iráklion.

Begin the walk at the newly built **taverna** at the end of the road. First continue to climb up the gravel road to the **Análipsi chapel** and then on the next long bend, turn off onto the *marked path*. Slowly going uphill across the mountainside to the south, the path turns right, northwards, into a cleft. The different signs alternate but you can follow the recent E4 waymarkers which you can see a long way off. At the top you have a good view of the valley bot-

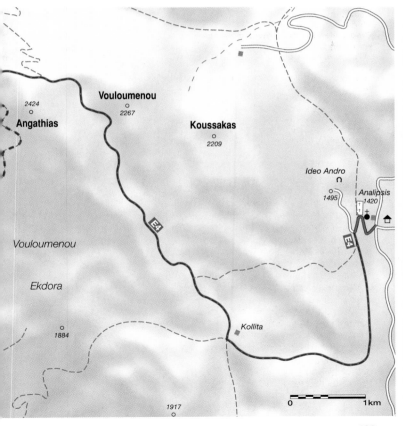

tom which is part of the Alp Kóllita and you climb down south-west towards this (about 100m). After 2¾ hrs. you join the ascent path from Kamáres. From the **Kóllita meadow** a long cleft goes high up to the north-west. After about 4¼ hrs. you go round a crater-like hole to the right, swing north-west and then keep left up to a col which goes west. Situated at 2456m in a stone hut, the **Tímios Stavrós chapel** marks the highest point of the Ida mountains which you now reach via its northern flank. Nearby there's a shelter and a cistern. The panorama is breathtaking – in the north the Cretan Sea, in the south the greenhouses of the Messará plain and the Libyan Sea and in the west the White Mountains. In the grey rocky landscape below to the south-west you can just see the mountain hut of the Réthimnon mountaineering club.

The return is far quicker. After 3 hrs. you are back on the Nídha plain and if you are lucky enough to be able to ski down some snow slopes, you will do it in even less time.

Right: the northern summit of Psilorítis.
Below: taking a rest on the way up to Psilorítis.

47 To the summit of Psilorítis from the south

Ascent of Psilorítis from Kamáres

Kamáres – Alp Kóllita – Tímios Stávros (Psilorítis)

Starting point: eastern end of Kamáres.
Walking time: Kamáres – Mándra Kalamáfka 1¾ hrs., Mándra Kalamáfka – vulture country 1½ hrs., vulture country – Alp Kóllita 1 hr., Alp Kóllita – Tímios Stavrós 2½ hrs, descent about 4½ hrs. Total time about 11½ hrs.
Ascent: 1800m.
Grade: sturdy footwear and clothing relative to the time of year. Fitness and good route finding ability required and surefootedness when crossing the snowfields in spring. Should be attempted only in stable weather. Very hot in summer.
Stops and accommodation: hotels in Kamáres and Zarós. A tent would be an advantage.
Alternatives: south-west descent alternative via the EOS hut to Kouroútes (see Walk 46). Eastern alternative via the Alp Kóllita to the Nídha plain. As a day walk as far as the vulture country and back.
Bus services: Iráklion – Míres – Kamáres.

The ascent of Psilorítis from Kamáres unfolds as a twisting alpine work of art. It is not only the considerable difference in height of 1800m which demands an appropriate fitness, but the sun too, which is relentless as you walk to the summit. But from the perspective of landscape this walk is one of the finest that the island of Zeus has to offer. The ever-present views down onto the Messará plain and the south coast are truly breathtaking.

And if you want to see the almost extinct lammergeier in flight, you are most likely to see them here. However, you should only undertake the walk during settled weather. Losing your way in the mist or falling down a crevice could have serious consequences. Otherwise the walk is not technically difficult and has sufficient waymarkers.

View down onto the Messará plain and the Libyan Sea.

Begin the walk, before sunrise if at all possible, at the eastern edge of **Kamáres** where a steep concrete track goes up (two red triangles in a white square). Further signs appear regularly. At the end of the concrete track go sharp right.

The path winds upwards essentially along a concrete water channel. After an hour you come to a tank with strongly bubbling water. After another hour on a well-marked path you come to a second water tank. You now find yourself in the area of the **Mándra Kalamáfka**. A Mándra means a shelter for shepherds or a simple pasture hut. Be careful to look out for the distinct waymarkers at this point where the path divides into two. Your path continues to the north onto the Psilorítis, the other one to the Kamáres cave more to the east. After the fork climb steeply upwards at the eastern edge of a deep gorge.

You are now surrounded by hazardous rock. 1½ hrs. after the Mándra Kalamáfka you come to the so-called **vulture spring** (Skarónero) on a hill at a height of 1650m. Thanks to the strict protection laws the number of lammergeier in this wild inaccessible area has risen again in the last few years. Three quarters of an hour after this you come to the shepherds' huts on the **Alp Kóllita**. Continue along the path to the north and you soon join the path coming up from the east from the Nídha plain. Now follow the path described in Walk 44 up to the top of **Psilorítis**. If you prefer not to take the same path back down you can also descend south westwards to Kouroútes on the Amári plain.

Below the summit to the south, above the tree line, you can see the mountain hut of the EOS Réthimnon (1498m, locked). From there it is about another 2½ hrs. down to Kouroútes.

48 From Kamáres to Kamáres cave

Throne of the gods suspended between heaven and sea

Kamáres – Mándra Kalamáfka – Kamáres cave

Starting point: eastern edge of Kamáres.
Walking time: Kamáres – Mándra Kalamáfka 1¾ hrs., Mándra Kalamáfka – Kamáres cave 1¼ hrs. Total time, including return, about 5 hrs.
Difference in height: 925m.
Grade: easy and well-marked paths.
Stops and accommodation: simple hotel in Kamáres. Better hotels in Zarós.
Alternative: from the Kamáres cave there are marked paths leading up to the southern end of the Nídha plain and down to Vorizia respectively.
Bus services: Iráklion – Míres – Kamáres.

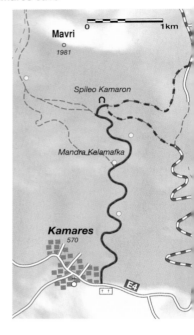

For those walkers who might shrink from the enormous climb onto the top of Psilorítis but would like to enjoy the beautiful view onto the Messará plain and the south coast of Crete, the Kamáres cave is a worthwhile alternative. That's what the ancient Minoans thought too when they discovered the cave as a place of worship situated between heaven and earth. In this truly heavenly spot the farmers from the Messará plain paid homage to the gods with the harvest. Remains of seeds, corn and crops were discovered in the pots found in the cave. The ornate pottery (1900 – 1700 B.C.) gave its name to a whole epoch (Kamáres style) and are on display in the Archaeological Museum in Iráklion.

You begin the walk at the eastern edge of **Kamáres** where a steep concrete track goes up (two red triangles in a white square). Further signs appear regularly. At the end of the concrete track go sharp right. The path winds upwards essentially along a concrete water channel. After an hour you come to a tank with strongly bubbling water. After another hour on a well-marked path you come to a second water tank which is part of the **Mándra**

Kalamáfka (Mándra = shepherds' shelter or simple mountain pasture). Shortly afterwards you come to a third tank (1280m) where some very visible waymarkers point the way to the Kamáres cave.

Turn off left here to the east and walk about 20 mins. by the side of a water pipe which leads to a stone reservoir called partridge water (**Perdhikónero**). 10 mins. later there's another tank. After a steep climb you can just make out, amongst the confusion of rocks, the dark entrance to the **Kamáres cave**. After 3 hrs. you are standing in the 42m wide and 19m high opening of the cave and as you look to the horizon and the sea you are aware of an aura of eternal godliness surrounding this place.

View out of the darkness of the Kamáres cave.

49 Roúwas gorge

Past trout ponds and picnic places into the Roúwas gorge

Zarós – Agios Nikólaos monastery – Roúwas gorge – Agios Ioánnis

Starting point: Zarós, road to the Idi hotel.
Walking time: ascent 2 hrs., descent 1½ hrs. Total time 3½ hrs.
Difference in height: 600m.
Grade: easy and impressive gorge walk on well-constructed path.

Stops and accommodation: tavernas in Zarós, trout specialities at the aquarium (by the Idi hotel) and Votómos (100m further on), overnight stop at Idi hotel, 700m from Zarós.
Bus services: Iráklion – Míres – Zarós.

When the ancient Cretans used to speak of Zarós they talked of richly bubbling springs which poured out from the mountains. Perhaps they also knew about the so-called 'Votomos' gorge (Roúwas gorge) and the pond formed from reeds not far from the lovely Nikólaos monastery. When the Cretans speak of Zarós today they immediately think of 'Pestrofa' which quite simply means trout. Although there have never been trout on Crete before, there has been a successful attempt to breed it in tanks full of oxygen. People come here on trips at the weekend and on public holidays to sample the unfamiliar freshwater fish in one of the fish tavernas. The previously reed-dammed pond is hardly recognisable today, so greatly has it been re-styled to make it attractive to tourists. Steps and wooden railings have made

A well-constructed path goes through the Roúwas gorge.

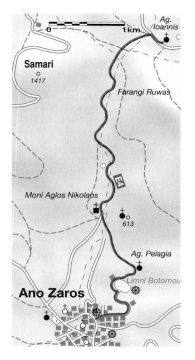

the path up into the gorge easier and safer. There's a pleasant place to picnic with benches and tables in the shade. The beautiful scenery of the Roúwas gorge is a popular day trip for walkers from as far away as Réthimnon. The only drawback is the walk through charred forest on your way up to the start of the gorge.

You reach the starting point of the walk by taking the road from **Zarós** to the **Idi hotel** (700m). Continue along the same road for 600m to the aforementioned **pond** with picnic tables. There are signposts pointing out the destinations and distances (0.9km to the Agios Nikólaos monastery, the length of the gorge 2.5km, 5.2km to the little church of Agios Ioánnis at the start of the plateau).

The **Agios Nikólaos monastery** can be reached in a quarter of an hour. Cross over to the other side of the stream by passing through the monastery, entering by its back gate. After half an hour you are back on the original side and you find a spring by the path. 5 mins. later, back in the streambed, you need to be careful. Do not proceed upwards in the streambed, go up the other side round a hairpin bend. You change sides a few more times, but the path is easy to follow.

You can see above the tops of the plane trees the towering rock faces where pines and cypress trees have taken root. In spring a little water finds its way through the smooth rocks of the streambed and wonderful pools and cascades are delightful places to bath. After 1¾ hrs. there's a pleasant place to sit and rest with tables and benches. From here it's just another 1.4km to the end of the walk which continues along the stream. After 2 hrs. you reach the edge of the plateau to find the little **Agios Ioánnis chapel**.

Huge old plane trees and oaks, an idyllic stream and green meadows all around perfect the idyll. A sign points to a cave 150m away where there is a memorial plaque.

50 Through the Roúwas gorge to the Gíristi

Gorge walk and mountain ascent in the Ida mountains

Zarós – Roúwas gorge – Gíristi

Starting point: Zarós, 350m, large tourist village south of the Ida massif.
Walking time: Zarós – Roúwas gorge – Agios Ioánnis 2 hrs., Agios Ioánnis – col 1¼ hrs., col – summit 1¼ hrs., return 3½ hrs. Total time 8½ hrs.
Difference in height: 1400m.
Grade: long mountain walk of moderate difficulty, lengthy sections ascending as well as descending on steep ground without paths.
Good footwear necessary.
Stops and accommodation: Idi hotel and rooms in Zarós. Many tavernas at the start of the walk catering for the coach loads of tourists.
Tip: Gortis near Agia Déka, Vrondissi and Valsamónero monasteries near Zarós.

This long but exceptionally beautiful walk shows off the characteristic contrasts of the islands. Start by driving along the road from Zarós to the Idi hotel and then a little further to the newly constructed lake where the walk actually begins (see Walk 47).
Directly above the **Agios Ioánnis chapel**, 950m, there's a roadway going up eastwards. The valley and the mountain slopes are densely covered with forests of oak trees. Go uphill gently for half an hour, mainly in the valley bottom next to a small stream. The road finally ascends on a wide right-hand bend onto the other side. If you like you can take a shortcut by following tracks right from the **valley bottom** straight up through the forest and meet the road again further up. The road zigzags its way steeply uphill and leads out onto an almost level terrace. Deeply indented cliffs, scree and prickly small oak trees shape the landscape. After almost 1½ hrs. you are standing at a junction on a flat **col** at a height of 1400m. The gravel road straight on leads down to Prínias across the bare mountainside, then goes right for a short way onto a higher col and left, crossing the Gíristi massif, into a large high valley where there's an extensive area of meadows.
You follow this road to the left and after 200m come past a large water tank. In the west the huge Psilorítis massif rises up with snowfields spreading over the summit region. About 300m after the water tank, a side valley leads up right. It is a steep and rather strenuous climb at first, and there are only goat paths to guide you to the top. Further up at 1500m there's a flat trough which you go round to the right and then, going north-eastwards, you come to a high flat ridge. The stone pyramid indicating 1640m is just ahead (30 mins.).
Continue across the broad ridge almost on a level, cross a deep hollow and finally you are climbing more steeply again over bands of rock to the summit of **Gíristi**, 1779m (45 mins.).

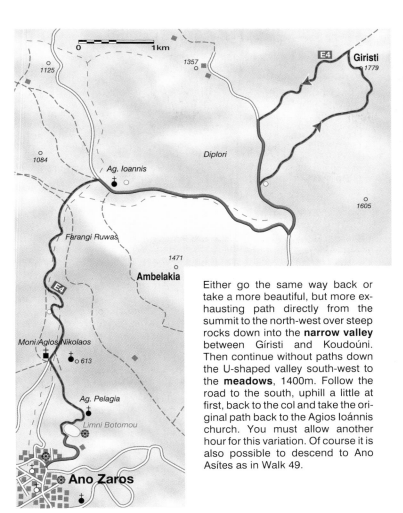

Either go the same way back or take a more beautiful, but more exhausting path directly from the summit to the north-west over steep rocks down into the **narrow valley** between Gíristi and Koudoúni. Then continue without paths down the U-shaped valley south-west to the **meadows**, 1400m. Follow the road to the south, uphill a little at first, back to the col and take the original path back to the Agios Ioánnis church. You must allow another hour for this variation. Of course it is also possible to descend to Ano Asítes as in Walk 49.

149

51 To the summit of Gíristi, 1779m

Views of vineyards and villages

Ano Asítes – Prínos hut – Gíristi

Starting point: Ano Asítes, 450m, small village 4km from Agia Varvára.
Walking time: Ano Asítes – Prínos hut 2 hrs., Prínos hut – Gíristi 2 hrs., return 2½ hrs. Total time 6½ – 7 hrs.
Difference in height: 1350m.
Grade: moderate mountain walk, across terrain without paths in places, easy climbing just before the summit, very hot in

summer, marvellous views from the most eastern summit of the Ida mountains.
Stops and accommodation: rooms in Agia Varvára, Ano Asítes and Agios Míronas, tavernas in all villages along the road.
Bus services: Iráklion – Ano Asítes several times a day.
Tip: Patéla near Prínias, excavations from Dorian times.

From Iráklion drive 25km to the village of **Ano Asítes** along the eastern foothills of the Ida mountains. After the last houses take the turn-off right onto a concrete road at first. A weathered wooden sign points the way to the *'Prínos hut EOS 1110m'* (key obtained from the EOS office in Iráklion). Following the yellow waymarkers go past some sheds, then left at each junction and the narrow road goes gently uphill in the shade of olive trees along a valley. After about 30 mins. cross over the stream on a narrow bend. After

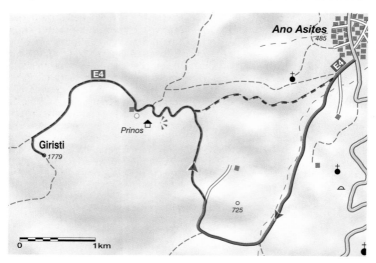

The rocky summit of Gíristi.

the fence blocking the road a red waymarker points along the streambed going upwards. This is a shortcut on a narrow path, but it's hard to find. So stay on the old trading route which leads up over bare open country round a wide bend towards a steep rocky ridge. At the next turn-off go left (the road to the right ends at the mountain hut you can see just a short way off) till it ends at a solitary tree. At another fence the red marked path comes up from the right. Now a path zigzags up through rocks to the top (yellow waymarkers). It leads into a cleft and reaches a flat terrace above. Dense undergrowth is evidence of a vigorous spring. 200m away further left the **Prínos hut** stands on a small plateau with fantastic views.

After a short stop, return to the path and ascend a narrow valley. After about half an hour (to the west) across a shallow hollow and past prickly bushes continue westwards following the line of the valley towards the rocky summit slightly over to the left above. Walk towards an ascending ridge and further left, after about 30 mins. you reach a small hollow. Finally climb up more steeply over rocks. A flat lengthy hollow going directly to the west is now ahead of you and a little left of it in the south-west you can clearly see the apparent summit pyramid of **Gíristi**. You easily reach the foot of the steep stone pyramid in 15 mins. and can start looking for a possible ascent route on the north side up to the flat summit plateau (20 mins.). Either return the same way or, as in Walk 50, descend the Roúwas gorge to Zarós (3½ hrs.).

The island of Gávdos

The delightful Potamós bay on the island of Gávdos.

Gávdos is not for ordinary tourists. You have to be a little mad to visit this arid barren island which lies 34 sea miles (55km) off the south coast of Crete. In the winter months boats carrying a maximum of 12 passengers only run twice a week and only then if the wind is no stronger than force 5. Any higher and you are stuck on the island with its 45 scattered inhabitants whose main occupation is sheep rearing. In summer bigger boats are deployed four times a week and they can hold up to 150 passengers. The journey from Paleohóra or Hóra Sfakíon to the port of Karáve takes just under 4 hrs. and a road runs from here up to the main village of **Kastrí** (1½ hrs. on foot or transport by tractor). The two other inhabited villages are **Ambelos** in the north-west and **Vatsianá** in the south. On the other hand the small island has 39 chapels – almost one per inhabitant. In Byzantine times when several thousand people lived on the island there was even a diocese here to which the villages of Sfakiá also belonged.

Historically there are a few puzzling things about the island. It is assumed that it is the island which, in the Odyssey, Homer calls Ogygia, where the seductive nymph Kalypso held the sailor from Ithaca hostage for seven years. The inhabitants of Gávdos are proud of a cave on the north-east point of the island which is supposed to be the nymph's palace. The Romans called the island Kauda. This is also the name of the island from which Saint Paul was driven away in the New Testament story (27, 16).

There's only water from cisterns on the 27 square metre island, or it is brought over from mainland Crete. The first site for the generation of solar energy is the island's new 'luxury', as well as ten telephone lines. The last little shop on Gávdos in Kastri was closed a few years ago. The fact that Gávdos is so irresistibly attractive to many people is due to its natural beauty, the deserted beaches, Aleppo pines twisted by the wind and juniper bushes. If you decide to make the jump to the most southern part of Europe a very special experience awaits you.

52 Round walk in the north of Gávdos

Idyllically beautiful beaches on the most southern island of Europe

Karáve – Sarakinikó beach – Laurakas beach – Pírgos beach – Potamós beach – Ambelos – Kastrí – Karáve

Starting point: Karáve.
Walking time: Karáve – Sarakinikó beach
½ hr., Sarakinikó beach – Laurakas beach
1 hr., Laurakas beach – Pírgos beach
1 hr., Pírgos beach – Potamós beach
1 hr., Potamós beach – Ambelos – Kastrí
1 hr., Kastrí – Karáve 1 hr.
Total time 5½ hrs.
Difference in height: 150m.
Grade: easy walk, but requiring stamina. Some need for route finding between Potamós and Ambelos. Take sufficient to drink.

Stops and accommodation: two tavernas with simple rooms in Karáve. Minimarket and tavernas on Sarakinikó beach during the season. Kafeníon in Kastrí.
Alternative: walk from Karáve to Kourfos or Trípiti in the south.
Boat services: in summer Paleohóra – Gávdos (4 hrs., Monday, Wednesday, Thursday, Friday, about 7,50 Euros), otherwise by small supply boats (maximum 12 passengers) Monday and Thursday. Hóra Sfakíon – Gávdos (2½ hrs. Saturday and Sunday).

The first stage of this coast walk takes you to Sarakinikó beach. At **Karáve** harbour go up the steps by the taverna on the left and you will come to a bend in the road. Just before on the left take the gravel road uphill and go along this road past 'Rooms Kalypso'. After 7 mins. you come to a turn-off to *'Kourfos beach'*, but continue straight on towards Sarakinikó beach. At the next fork go left towards Kastrí and then right to Sarakinikó beach. 10 mins. later there's another fork, straight on to *'Agios Giannis'* and right to Sarakinikó beach. The dry landscape is covered with pine and juniper trees. Before you reach **Sarakinikó beach** in just under half an hour your attention is drawn to some dreadful concrete huts. These are the converted buildings for the diesel generators which provide electricity to the ten simple beach tavernas. Some of the huts are already equipped with solar energy. Fine sand covers the delightful beach where an uncomplicated beach life is to be found. During the hot summer months the juniper trees just above, with their branches making tree-topped caves, offer the international beach sleeping community a roof under the starlit sky.

The path to Potamós beach begins on the western, left-hand side of Sarakinikó beach. Go uphill the gravel road as far as a natural stone house with green doors. Take the roadway behind it to the right (wire fence) along the coast. After half an hour the path forks and you go right. The path ends at a dry riverbed. Continue along the coast over the cliffs which are relatively safe to walk over, but without paths. After an hour you come to the hill with the Agios Geórgios chapel lying above the so-called **Laurakas** beach. A cliff path begins above at the end of the beach (surefootedness required). After

15 mins. continue along the shore again. Under the large juniper trees you find again and again the remnants of summery Robinson Crusoe style adventures. If it weren't for the nearby sea it would now appear as if you were going through a desert landscape. Red dunes, strange sandstone markings caused by biting winds, boulders full of holes and all the rubbish of civilisation with its plastic containers washed up by the sea and lastly the tar from which even these shores are not safe. Especially now, when we come round the northern point, the slabs appear as if covered in asphalt. After the ruins of a stone house ascend an older eroded path, about 2m broader, with a beautiful view across the cliffs of the sandy **Pírgos** bay. The path now turns inland towards Kastrí. In the distance, up on the left, the Agios Geórgios chapel stands out against the blue sky. Do not continue on this path. Go round Pírgos beach instead (3 hrs. up till now), along the cliffs above it until, in 20 mins., you can see **Potamós beach**, a red sandy bay reaching deep inland with a backdrop of a rocky landscape eroded by gullies.

Go round the bay at its highest point. At the top there are the ruins of stone houses with their former terraces below. You are standing on the edge of a gorge. Decorative patterns have been drawn onto the opposite rock face like symbols of a secret script (4 hrs.). A path goes from the ruins to the south (with your back to the ruins and Agios Geórgios), through a gate and left along a fence until a path stands out in the desert-like countryside and leads towards a house with solar panels on a hillside in the distance (right). You might need to find your own way through because of new fencing. It's a surprise to find so many weathered terraces. Were 7,000 people really supposed to have lived here?

In front of the house which belongs to the hamlet of **Ambelos**, a gravel road goes eastwards. After 5 mins. you go through a gate. Another 5 mins. after the gate a distinct path crosses the road. Turn right onto this path and follow it through pine trees as it runs along the right-hand side of the road and then rejoins the road. After 5 hrs., before the first house in **Kastrí** with a conspicuous aerial, go left at the fork and left again at the next fork. The roadway then leads between two chapels (on the right Panagía, on the left Christós). Below there's a forest of tall pines. Continue along the roadway and finally, weary after an extremely long walk, return to your starting point in Karáve.

Index

THE GREEK ALPHABET

Αα	Aa	Ββ	Bb	Χχ	Gg	Δδ	Th	Εε	Ee	Ζζ	Zz
Ηη	Jj	Θθ	Th	Ιι	Jj	Κκ	Kk	Λλ	Ll	Μμ	Mm
Νν	Nn	Ξξ	Xx	Οο	Oo	Ππ	Pp	Ρρ	Rr	Σσ	Ss
Ττ	Tt	Υυ	Ii	Φφ	Ff	Χχ	Ch	Ψψ	Ps	Ωw	Oo

Geographical

jeojrafikós chartis	road map
póli	town
chorió	village
spíti, spítia	house, houses
eklissía, eklissáki	church, chapel
dhromos	road / street
monopáti	path
strofí	bend
stavrodhrómi	wayside cross
wunó	mountain
katariji	mountain hut
korifí	summit
hióni	snow
petres	stones
farángi	gorge
spiljá	cave
pedhiáda	plain
potamós	river
límni	lake
thálassa	sea
pijí	spring
dhéndhro, dhásos	tree, forest
lulúdhi	flower
prówata	sheep
katzíkes	goats
skílos	dog
pulí	bird

Food, accomodation and transport

xenodhochío	hotel
krewáti	bed
lutró, dus	bath, shower
faí	food
psomí	bread
kréas	meat
psári	fish
tirí	cheese
féta	feta cheese
frúta	fruit
eliés	olives
ládhi	oil
aláti	salt
pipéri	pepper
neró	water
krasí	wine
chimós	juice
kafés	coffee
tsai	tea
hiliómetro	kilometre
avtokínito	car
leoforío	bus
isitírio	ticket
stási	bus stop

General phrases

woíthia	help
parakaló? oríste	please
evcharistó	thank you!
signómi	sorry
kaliméra	hello
kaliníchta	good night
adhío	goodbye
símera	today
ávrio	tomorrow
chtes	yesterday
póte?	when?
pu?	where?
póso?	how much?
ti?	what
makriá	far
kontá	near
psilá	high
hamilá	low
káto	below
páno	above
krio	cold
sestó	warm
fotinó	light / bright
skótino	dark
ftinó	cheap
akriwó	expensive